SECRETS to SERENE SPACE

ART OF SPACE CLEARING
CLEAR NEGATIVE ENERGIES
USE METAPHYSICS AND
AFFIRMATIONS TO CHANGE
YOUR SPACE AND LIFE

MYRA SRI

Energy Healing Secrets Series: 5

Copyright and Legal Notice

This Book is Copyright © 2014 and Beyond: Myra Sri (the 'Author'). All rights reserved worldwide.

Reproduction or translation of any part of this work beyond that permitted by section 107 or 108 of the 1976 United States Copyright Act without permission of the copyright owner is unlawful. Requests for permission or further information should be addressed to the Author. No part of this eBook may be translated or reproduced or transmitted in any form or by any means, electronic or mechanical, including photocopying, recording, or by an information storage and retrieval system without the express permission of the Author.

This publication is designed to provide accurate and Authoritative information in regard to the subject matter covered, based on the Author's experience, research, practice and understandings. The Author and publisher do not recommend anything contrary to common sense. If professional medical or nutritional advice or other expert assistance is required, the services of a competent professional person should be sought.

First Published as an electronic book in Australia 2015

First Printing, **September 2015**

Published by Healing Knowhow Publishing,

Suite 2/36 Wallarah Rd, Gorokan, NSW 2263, Australia

National Library of Australia Cataloguing-in-Publication entry:
Sri, Myra, author
Secrets to serene space : art of space clearing; clear
negative energies, use metaphysics and affirmations
to change your space and life / Myra Sri
ISBN: 978-0-9923924-5-1 (paperback)
Energy healing secrets series ; 5
Personal space
Metaphysics
304.23

Books by the Same Author

Energy Healing Secrets Series

Secrets Beyond Aromatherapy

Secrets Behind Energy Fields

Secret Truths to Health and Well-Being

Crystal Codes – Align to the New Incoming Energies

Guided Meditations at www.myrasri.com/new-healing-store

Amazon Series Reviews:

"Thrilled with the content of this book and I have read almost every aromatherapy book there is"

"I wonder why this book is not used as a textbook"

"Thanks to this eBook, I am teaching myself to rise above the conflict at work… these life skills are priceless!"

"This is an excellent, practical, down to earth book that is filled with simple techniques to get in touch with yourself, your own energy, what is affecting it and then how to do something about it."

"I found this book very informative and the techniques were simple and easy to follow. I would recommend it to anyone who does energy work."

Acknowledgements

Thank you to my clients, students and colleagues for your encouragement to share my knowledge with a wider audience.

***

CONTENTS

INTRODUCTION 11
THE WHAT, WHY, WHEN, WHERE & HOW OF SPACE CLEARING 15
    Serenity AND Fun! 16
The "What" Of Space Clearing 17
    Stagnation 18
    Coming Unstuck 19
    Simplicity 21
    Assess 23
    Definitions of Space Clearing: 25
    Difference between Space Clearing and Feng Shui ... 25
Space Clearing Mission 29
    What is Meant by "Space"? 29
    What is Meant by "Clearing"? 30
    What is Meant by Energetic Clearing? 34
Why Do Space Clearing? 37
    The Human Factor 39
    Benefits of Space Clearing 41
    What Needs Space Clearing? 42
    When To Do Space Clearing 45
The "How" - Space Clearing Techniques 47
    Define the Problem/s 47
    Define the Space 48
    The Process And Intention Of Space Clearing 49
    Visualisation – Free, Easy, Repeatable 50
PLACES AND SPACES 53
    New Home 53
    Geographic Relocation 54
    Work Place Issues 59
    Vehicles 60
    Hospitals / Waiting Rooms 61
THE COMPLETE SPACE CLEARING PROCESS 63

   Preparation For Clearing 63
      Prepare Yourself! 63
      Assemble Your Tools! 64
      Space Clearing Kits 64
   Full Space Clearing Treatment 65
   QUICK mini Clearing 67
ESSENTIAL AIDS TO CLEARING **69**
   Pendulum 69
      How to Use a Pendulum 70
      Testing the Space 73
   DE-CLUTTER 75
      What it is and How to Do It 75
      Do It Yourself Declutter 77
      Finish off your Declutter 79
      FENG SHUI 81

TOOLS FOR SPACE CLEARING AND ENHANCING **89**
      Affirmations 90
      Artwork and Calligraphy 90
      Boundaries 92
      Brass Bowls 94
      Bucket 95
      Burning-Off 95
      Candles 97
      Cd Player 98
      Ceremony 99
      Chimes 103
      Clapping 104
      Clear Drains 106
      Color 107
      Crystals And Stones 109
      Energy Fields 110
      Essential Oils 111

Feng Shui Tips 113
Fabrics, Furnishings 114
Furniture Clearing 115
Gratitude Exercise 116
Hair Clearing 117
Hanging Mobiles 118
House-Warming Party 119
Imprints 121
Incense 123
Invocations 124
Jugments and Labels 124
Lavender Oil Furniture Polish 124
Lost Souls / Earthbounds 126
Mantras / Chants 127
Mattress Clearing 129
Methylated Spirits 131
Mirror 132
Mobiles 134
Music 135
Musical / Sound Instrument 136
Objects 137
Orbs 138
Paint 139
Portals 140
Pyramid 141
Reclaim / Reset / Infill 143
Rituals / Ceremonies 144
Room By Room 145
Sage Sticks / Herbs 146
Salts – Sea / Rock / Epsom 147
Satin and Beautiful Fabric 148
Smudging 149
Sounds / Noise 150

  Sprays 151
  Spring Cleaning 153
  Symbol / Mandala 154
  Travel Spray 156
  Tv, Computers 156
  Ultra-Violet 157
  Vacuuming and Sweeping 158
  Walls 160
  Washing and Cleaning 161
  Zen 163

STATEMENTS SECTION 165
AFFIRMATIONS TO CLEAR 166
  Drains 169
  Earthbounds & Lost Souls 169
  Emotions 170
  Electrical / Electronic Energy Imprints 170
  Entities 171
  Fragmented Energies 171
  Guardians 171
  Hoarding 172
  Imprints 172
  Others Belongings 172
  Orbs 173
  Portals 173
  Residues 173
  Thoughtforms 173
AFFIRMATIONS FOR CHANGE 175
  The Statements 176

WHAT NOW? WHAT NEXT? 179
  Easy Repeat 181
FURTHER INFORMATION 183
  About the Author 185

Introduction

You know those times when you have been out, possibly travelling or have been busy helping a friend, or doing something that has taken you away from home and loved ones, and you have had to either be alert, or on your guard or wary, or just been kept continually on the go? And then you come home to find your own personal place refreshed and tidy, with a familiar essence about the place that is friendly and warm and pleasant? And you finally feel that you can let your guard down, be yourself again, rest and recover, relax and refresh?

Imagine that feeling right now – play it over in your body – feel and see it happening...

That's right. You go *HOME*! It *feels* like home. It feels that it's *yours*. It feels safe, and welcoming, and you feel cared for and loved. You feel that it is a place to recover in, to nurture and reenergize yourself. The air feels clear, things feel fresh and clean, and *welcoming*. There is nothing to make you feel anxious again, you can let that all go! Everything you require to help you feel good about yourself, good about life, good about work, is all there for you!

What a great feeling!

This is how it feels to find *Sanctuary*, to be yourself again, to be *Home*.

Now THAT is a great space to be in.

Now remember the times you have visited someone and felt uncomfortable being in their place. Or in some other space that wasn't yours. And you couldn't wait to get away. Or remember those times that you have come home to your own space, and things have felt yucky even there. Or maybe someone has just visited you that makes you feel like crap after they leave. And the place now seems to have some kind of smell to it which wasn't there before. And it's not related to food or dirty washing left lying around. You feel invaded. Frustrated. *Unhappy*.

Or you have just seen something on the television or video that now seems to have penetrated into the very air and atoms in the house. And you don't quite feel safe or certain any more. And you wonder how you can get rid of this sense of despair or fear again. Even after you tidy up, you feel anxious and just can't relax. And you know that it is not necessarily you or your feelings that is causing this, it just *is*, in the room.

Your space has been invaded. The vibrations are no longer harmonious and this can be from a variety of causes. And this can happen to anyone at any time.

Take a look around your room, around the place you sleep in and eat in and come back to in order to recharge, to rest up or simply to get away from everyone.

How does it feel?

Welcoming? Happily personal?

A pleasure to be in that makes you feel really good about yourself? A place in which to express yourself? A place to feel safe?

If it doesn't feel like this, then why not?

Has someone or something else taken over your place and space in any way? Taken over control of your life? Or have you let it go yourself?

Have you taken care of the space which is supposed to take care of You?

Your home reflects you. It reflects how you feel about yourself. It also reflects what you allow to happen in your life. It may even reflect what you are not prepared to look at, but which follows you in energetically even so.

But...

What if you *knew* how to fix this, and do it quickly?

What if you could reclaim your living space and connect back to feeling nurtured again? What if old energies and wandering unsupportive new energies could be cleared out for good? What if you could again choose to experience Serenity in your place again? Or to feel energized and happy and again want to entertain those people that you care about and that care for you?

This is all part of Space Clearing. And this book will show you how to reclaim your space and peace of mind again. Easily and safely.

In this book you will find expert and effective techniques that will help you to clear and re-establish your space again as well as give you tools to ensure you have covered all your bases.

The What, Why, When, Where & How Of Space Clearing

Space Clearing has generally and more often than not been done by experts in a professional capacity. And sometimes, this is a good thing. However, there are several different levels to Space Clearing, and not all professionals know all there is to know about it - *and* there is so much that can be done by oneself – *when* one knows *how*!

The questions that need to be answered are:

WHAT, WHY, WHEN, WHERE???

& HOW!!

So to begin we already know that the *WHO* is *YOU*!

You are a major key to creating a new sense in your personal space.

This is your domain, your territory. And you are the one who has the power to clean out what you do not wish to invade your home.

Getting clear that you do not need things in your space that attract crappy energy, that makes you feel older than you are, that unnerves you and makes you feel uncomfortable and uneasy, or that tends to attract "stuff" that we eventually find it hard to wade through... this is an important step in being able to change how we see not only our space, but ourself.

We will be looking at not only how other people, other things beyond our seeming control affect our place, but also what it is that we contribute to all of this. This is a chance to not only reclaim your place and space for you to be more of who you are, but also to recover "home" – the place where you go to recover, to refresh, to renew, to find peace. And sometimes to lick one's wounds and to heal.

Here is a huge collection of tools, ideas, suggestions and background information to assist you in Space Clearing – and to give you the tools of the *Experts*!

I have been working with energy for many, many years, and it took me quite a while to understand that not only *where* we work with energy, but also *how* we work with energy is of prime importance in not only energy or healing work, but also in keeping our home space and living spaces clear and supportive.

Serenity AND Fun!

When serenity reigns at home, we rejuvenate and heal. A serene space doesn't mean not having any parties or fun times, it means that the energy of the space and place is free from harsh or distracting energies, frequencies or vibrations that cause our heart to race, or our nerves to fray.

This book covers just about everything to do with Space Clearing, and helps you to get clear what you need to do to experience the joy of a supportive and energizing space.

THE "WHAT" OF SPACE CLEARING

The idea of Space Clearing is not a new one, though **how** we go about it may have differed somewhat over time. There are various aspects to clearing an environment, and sometimes we need to examine just **what** it is we are doing, exactly what is required, what we want to achieve, and ... *what it is that we don't-yet-know-about that could make-all-the-difference...?*

When asked, a variety of people have said what Space Clearing means to them. This includes the following general ideas and comments:

tidying up, moving furniture to make more space, smudging with a smudge stick, getting rid of ghosts, burning incense or something similar, Feng Shui, making the place feel better, moving on of "heavy energies", throwing stuff out etc.

Well, this covers some aspects. But is it enough? Is it a true picture of Space Clearing? In some cases, the answer is Yes. In others, the answer would be No.

Space clearing is after all about clearing the *ENERGY! Changing* the energy!

Most people with an understanding of energy and things energetic will think of it in terms of those things we cannot see but which we can feel, or which impact on how we feel and also how we function in any given space.

It can be all of these and much more.

The loveliest of homes can unexpectedly have dramatic, upsetting or terrible things happen in them, and those who live there can find that the resulting negative energies can affect the ambience and feel or energy of the place for many years after. And similar upsetting or awkward or negative energies may also enter or be carried in from outside quite accidentally at any time.

The secret to maintaining a supportive space is in knowing **how** to get rid of these!

This can happen no matter if you live in a humble abode or a luxury mansion.

Stagnation

They can also accumulate where there is stagnation – where things have stopped moving naturally and have become stymied or stuck. Most of us know what happens when the main domestic carer is incapacitate or taken ill or away caring for someone else – and this can be our self if we live alone. Things just don't get done. Stuff builds up. We don't have the strength or energy to sort everything out for our self.

I remember breaking a wrist and being in a cast for six weeks. It also took a further several weeks to get full movement back again. I could not have managed without a couple of friends bringing over soup occasionally, or doing some of my accumulating dishes. Bathing difficulty was another problem I won't even attempt to explain.

Things mounted up amazingly quickly, newspapers, mail, dishes, rubbish, dust… I was itching – literally – to put things back where they belonged, to move things out of my way again, to sort through. But because I was recovering, I was in no place to be able to attempt these things. I was exhausted from dealing with life at the time, and this may well have been a subconscious way of having the rest I needed (I will never ever say to myself or anyone else again that "I need a break" because I certainly got it!) and the trauma of the break created further issues for my body to deal with and heal.

But it gave me time to consider many things. And to see how well my space worked for me when I needed it to.

As soon as I was well again, I made the changes I needed and I reveled in the feeling of the place feeling like mine again, feeling like a home again instead of a hospital.

It gave me time to consider what really mattered. I realized I didn't really like the paintings on my wall, and decided that when I was able I would paint my own pictures and hand them up no matter how they turned out. They would be colorful, and make me feel happy or make me feel serene – that was my prime objective. Though in actual fact, it took me several go's to feel happy about permanently looking at my first one. Soon after I found I had done several paintings and was even getting happy compliments! What a surprise! But more importantly, it allowed me to claim the wall space as mine, to discover what made me happy, to express myself and to be more of who I was.

Coming Unstuck

Decluttering is a first and basic step to bringing more energy movement into any place. Working out what matters, what is current, what is supportive and in doing so, then taking action on this will not only help to clear one's space, but also help to clear one's mind and emotions.

Sometimes we get stuck emotionally – we fear feeling something that is hurtful or fearful. Or we can even fear feeling the opposite of that again – in case we wind up the same way; losing it. We may choose to deal with something in a way that doesn't really deal with it: we may deny it, suppress it, see it through sentimental eyes, hold onto the hurt so tightly that we numb ourselves, we may hold a grudge, add it to our "list" of hurts or offences, or a whole number of ways that are possible.

However, this doesn't serve us.

I believe that we must allow the process of grieving for something that we have lost in order to be able to accept our new situation and then be able to move on. If we pretend that nothing is wrong, that things are fine and that there is no effect on us, yet we have buried it so far within so that we cannot feel it, this may give a temporary space, but the energy is still there.

We are not free of it until we are free from it.

The success of space and energy clearing and energy flow in a home is always linked to the flow of energy within the owner, if the clearing is not simply because we are now in new premises.

So without further adding to your own self criticism or judgments, or to your feeling of stuck-ness, now is the time to *be kind* to yourself. And to realize just what it is you have been holding onto, or allowing, and to *begin* to be willing (there is actually a process for some people in these words) – yes, begin to be *willing* to give *yourself* permission to deal with whatever it is, to heal whatever it is and to move on from whatever it is.

If you don't know how to do this, the first thing, as I mentioned, is to be *willing* to begin the process. This change in thought will allow new ways of looking at things to begin to bring toward you what it is you need to deal with to really and fully move on. Working on your home space can also help activate this same forward movement in one's energy, in one's intentions.

"Thought flows where energy goes."

What you focus on begins to happen. Wherever you put your attention, energy follows that and further adds to it. Whatever you give your attention to will increase in time. So taking focus off what you cannot do, and placing your attention on finding what it is you *can* do, right then, will begin this change in direction of your energies.

So if you know you have been stuck somewhere, now that you have begun to be kind to yourself, and to begin to be willing to give yourself permission to do whatever it takes to get through this in a kind supportive way to yourself, let us look at the options to do so.

As I mentioned earlier, decluttering a space is always a good starter. So begin by throwing out what you no longer need, what only brings you pain, what keeps you stuck, what holds you back, what no longer brings you pleasure, and what you hold onto because of duty.

Let it go!

I will give you that list again:

> *Throw out what you no longer need*
>
> *Get rid of what only brings you pain*
>
> *Recognize and remove what keeps you stuck*
>
> *Release what holds you back*
>
> *Say goodbye to that which no longer gives you pleasure*
>
> *Remove those things you have looked after or held onto through pure duty – give them back – let them go!*
>
> *Rethink what it is you want in your Sanctuary – what now really matters to you? What helps you to feel good about yourself, what frees up your space for you to live again?*

Simplicity

I have listed some affirmations at the back of the book if you wish to use them for further self development, for further informing your mind and heart the direction you wish to take. Or to help you move into a space that allows you to let go or to move forward again. You can also use these to meditate with or if you do energy work of any kind (by yourself or with a practitioner or therapist) to move you forward faster.

Decluttering the mind and heart, removing the blocks there if there are any will speed up your process. Those of you who do not necessarily have any real psychological or emotional work to do will probably find there is little to declutter. But maybe there is a new view of life to be gained by reassessing the space and the placement of items in that space for flow and ease of movement.

I have heard it said that the Zen psychology is built on function – only have something if you really need it. But Zen function is also built on aesthetics – it doesn't jar the senses, it supports the spirit. Zen simplicity seems to combine beauty or design with function. This is something to keep in mind that may assist in decisions as to what to have where. Zen certainly allows for movement, leaving space in a room and environment – the sort of space that seems to draw in good energy and also seems to draw us out of ourselves.

Zen is about living simply. I like to think that after having a fire which destroyed everything I had except the two suitcases I had with me, that I now live far more simply than before. Gone are the range of crystal glasses, the casseroles in case I had a huge party, gone are lots of trimmings for so many things that never happened. I live functionally now, though I chose my effects very carefully. And I get pleasure from what I have been able to match up with what. And what does double duty. Having said that, my kitchen is happy, reasonably clear, yet things are to hand quickly. Not at all the same clutter as I had in my cupboards before the fire – too much "stuff". There is not much wall cupboard space where I live now, none in fact at all, but I have a couple of shelves that serves to hold my happy functional but attractive mugs and matching storage jars. A couple of white wicker basket type boxes on the shelf holds my nutritional supplements in a tidy way, and are easy to pick up for use, as well as easy on the eye.

I live much more minimally now, and even though I have begun to accumulate paints and canvases again, they occupy only a small space in my place. And I actually have what is called "surfaces" – flat spaces that I can bring things out and place them upon to use them and then put them away again. Only rarely do I realize that I am running out of space and then I have to clear away objects from one activity to allow another. But all of this keeps the energy moving in my space. And brings me variety, color and enjoyment when I require it.

Yes, if I had a large house with lots of rooms that I could dedicate to different tasks, I could spread out. But for me, it would mean so much more work, and cleaning, and (knowing myself from old) more accumulation and more work – meaningless enjoyment of what I had. So I am happy with this arrangement. This works for me.

Now find out what works for you!

What things would you like to bring out that feeds your soul? What things dare you release that you no longer need?

Assess

Assess your place, your space. Does it need a declutter first? Do you need to release something? Do you need to replace it with something? From your home, your heart, your mind?

Assessment is the first step – what does your home need? Later I also show you how to assess the movement of energy within a room.

Does your home simply need Feng Shui?

Does it need clearing of negative energy and thus need a Space Clearing?

There is obviously a direct relationship between Space Cleansing or Clearing and Feng Shui, but they are not necessarily the same thing.

Space Clearing can cleanse the space, and Feng Shui can assist with creating a better energy flow which can help to prevent stagnant energies from building up again. Feng Shui alone may be insufficient to cleanse a heavy energetic space, and Space Clearing alone may not be enough to help prevent and repel a certain level of negative energy occurrences. Both can work together very well. And you don't have to be an expert with either to achieve a measure of success and greatly improve a space, if you know *HOW*.

But there is further step to this I would like to cover – and that is to reset the energies and to not only *take out* the energies that you *don't want*, but also to take care to *put in* the energies that you *do want*.

If you have found that decluttering or Feng Shui is not enough, or your current Space Clearing ideas aren't working effectively, then this book is for you.

Definitions of Space Clearing:

Here are some common definitions of Space Clearing from a variety of sources, as well as my own:

- The removal of toxic build-up in a living or working space
- The release of stuck energies that no longer serve us
- The removal or detoxification of unseen energies that can invade or affect the ambience of a place, space or location
- The art of clearing and consecrating energies in buildings and living spaces
- Energy maintenance of a site similar to physical cleaning and maintenance but on an energetic level
- The enhancement and improvement of an area including the energy in it
- A ceremony intended to rid a building of poor or overpowering energies
- A type of house blessing
- A dedication of a living or working space to a higher purpose
- The clearing of unwanted unsupportive energies and the setting of boundaries to prevent unwanted energetic intrusions
- The establishing of preferred and supportive harmonious energies

Difference between Space Clearing and Feng Shui

Feng Shui

Feng Shui (*fung shway*) is the Art and Practice of Energy Movement.

Developed over many centuries in China, it is still practiced there today, and is mostly always taken into consideration by their architects, builders and renovators alike. It is concerned with lay-out, design, function and placement for the best energy flow effect. It is often practiced in many other countries now, becoming not only a maintenance and aesthetic application but often part of current architect design. Though not always. As is demonstrated by some really sharply pointed corners on some buildings that can have a negative impact on the buildings in the path of such lines.

Feng Shui can include de-cluttering (of objects, possessions, furnishings or memorabilia), some enhancing or embellishing (plants, mirrors, pictures, color etc), design (elegance and simplicity in layout, architecture, décor and furnishing), the abstract (with a focus on the astrological, numerological indications of the house number of the property and the owners / occupiers) and geological location positioning and significances.

Positioning considerations can include terrain and geography (valleys, obstructions to view, nearby hills, river flows or mountains etc) and directional considerations (North, South etc). Elemental aspects representing aspects of fire, wind, air, water etc are considered and can include bodies or containers of water, wind chimes, metal, flowers, crystals or other energy or chi components that denote, symbolize or encourage life force and fresh energy or vitality.

The focus is usually primarily built on awareness and deliberations of art, energy distribution and aesthetics (sometimes in a scientific application) that can include certain recognized guidelines of placement, visual appearance and the esoteric.

Space Clearing

Space Clearing is may be seen at one end of the scale as a form of refurbishment and restyling, a way of clearing old materials from a space or at the other extreme as a form of exorcism of ghosts etc. In its true sense it is actually the art of clearing negative, intrusive, destructive, stagnant or other interfering energies from a space so that vital energy can support the occupiers, and so that they can be in their own energy space so to speak. Space Clearing is generally primarily concerned with the energetic feeling, ambience and energy clarity of a place, space or dwelling.

This seems to be approached from a different perspective to Feng Shui, one that is built on a sense of unseen energetic clarity, a lifting of negative energies and imprints, or the removal of heavy or inharmonious energies. This may not necessarily require removal of or the re-placement or relocation of items of furniture. In fact there may be hardly any need at all for placement of furniture alterations after the removal of "toxic" energies. Though one may well find that the best solution can be a combination of both practices, depending on the need of the space itself.

There can be several levels to Space Clearing, depending on the level of current toxicity of a given spot or position. Feng Shui may also be included as a consideration to enhance the Space Clearing work.

Both approach the enhancement of a space though both come from different viewpoints, and using different techniques. But they can complement each other when applied appropriately.

Feng Shui and Space Clearing Used Together

The purity of a space can often be beautified and assisted with Feng Shui principles. Feng Shui may often be considered more as a prevention, rather than a cure, if applied appropriately to the site. Though it is wise to interpret according to the hemisphere of the world one is living or working in, as meanings and effects can change between northern and southern hemispheres depending on the particular interpretation and teaching of the type of Feng Shui pursued. It has been noted that the astrological aspects don't always work exactly the same (everywhere) in every case, due to the disparity between interpretation and understanding of Western, Chinese and Vedic Astrologies. So allow yourself to intuit what is best for you.

Feng Shui alone may not be enough, yet certain aspects may be used to support space clearing.

The intention of Space Clearing will *Always* be to enhance a site or situations purity and clarity. The clearing of energies is often experienced as the feel of clean air after a cleansing rain or a long-awaited thunderstorm.

SPACE CLEARING MISSION

Let us get really clear of what we want to achieve and put the phrase "Space Clearing" into simple and understandable terms.

But just before we do, let us mention that in essence it is the art of cleansing and healing the energy held within buildings, as well as being a respectful practice for raising and stabilizing the vital energy within a building or property. And it should free up previously "heavy" and stagnant spaces.

Space Clearing – Is the clearing of unwanted unsupportive energies, the enhancing of energetic vitality and harmony and the setting of boundaries to discourage further unwanted energetic intrusions within a given area.

Good Space Clearing should also bring with it a sense of space, order and clarity. And in most cases, a feel of success, love or at very least, of serenity.

What is Meant by "Space"?

Space in the context of Space Clearing can mean a room, a building, an office, a house or home, an area, a site or any geographical location usually inhabited, used or visited by people or beings (may include animals). We are obviously not referring to outer space where the Planets and stars reside.

Space here then would mean physical areas that provide freedom, liberty, legroom and all related movement in situations that include geographical areas such as a place, dwelling or vehicle..Or even a clearing in an open field for the purposes of a group outing or celebration.

It includes not just the physical walls, flooring and ceilings, but also the area of atmosphere, zone or space that is included within and sometimes, without or around the physical structure.

We sometimes talk about the need or desire for more "headspace", leg space, personal space, breathing space, room to move and other similar idioms that say we feel cramped or crammed or hemmed in. This can apply to the energy or atmospheric area that we feel deprived or short of, and we feel it in a physical way. Our space is very important then, to how we feel about life, or work, or about our self.

An employee or worker in a largish office with an outside window often feels more expansive, productive, appreciated, rewarded and happier than someone crowded into a tiny working space with little freedom, light or privacy. Open work places do not suit every occupation by a long shot, though some jobs do call for this type of intimate proximity for the immediacy of communication. In these instances, personal boundaries and energetic boundaries may need some attention.

We can also include our car or motor vehicle or any other regular space we occupy or utilize that we can have some degree of control over.

What is Meant by "Clearing"?

On the physical level, it can mean the removal of unwanted, outworn or unnecessary items. This is often referred to as an Un-Cluttering or a De-Clutter / declutter.

Then we address what we cannot see. These are the things beyond the immediately visual or physical. The things that impact on a space, be they memories, or a "sense" of things or a "feel" to things. An idea that it may not be as it should or that it could feel much better than it does.

Clearing a space has several levels and if you wish, they could be separated into these following areas, steps, understandings or stages.

First Stage

The first step then, is to declutter, to see what we furniture, objects or materials that we really need, what we will or still use, what "fits" in our newly defined space, and also to get rid of what no longer works for us or supports us.

This sorting and tidying and rearranging or removal of refuse and of the unnecessary is often the first stage of a Space Clearing, the very physical stage, and usually begins a creating of order – it is the start of the ordering and organizing process.

There is a very real parallel to this step – and that is that while we are decluttering in this very physical manner, we are also, on some level of our being, sorting out within our hearts, minds or subconscious, those things that we no longer want or need in our lives. We are in fact "lightening-up" our selves, as well as our environment, letting go of that which is no longer supportive, useful or required. Whenever we feel the need to move things around, to create a new order out of our environment, we are signaling those inner steps we are taking with regard to old or existing attitudes in our lives. It is usually always a good sign to want to "sort" out our environment.

Second Stage

The second aspect is the attention to the "feel", ambience or atmosphere within the physical confines of the place or space. If a room has been locked up for a long while, for instance, there will be a sense of stagnation, which may still persist even after the dust has been removed, and light or air (via the opening of doors, windows, curtains or blinds) has been allowed to enter. Objects in the room will still retain some of the "stagnant" energies as well as some history of the object.

This then, on an inner level, can signal our desire to allow more light, more energy, more vitality into our lives and our experiences. This can also indicate our allowing a better clarity and recognition on what we encounter in life may improve our response or reactions to these encounters.

Third Stage

If there has been a trauma, shock, or deep emotional event in the place, this can impact and affect the energy of the room too, until dealt with.

So the third aspect is the more deeply ingrained energetic imbalances that prevent harmony, peace, happiness or a sense of freedom within the place or space.

On an inner level, this can mirror or signal to us a desire that we are willing to let go of old pains. This is because when you remove an energetic "trigger" from a room, such as a very painful experience in your past, you are helping to remove your attachment to the painful memory associated with it. This then can help to allow you to move on in life.

Fourth Stage

There is a fourth aspect, that of unseen energies that are more deeply ingrained, though fortunately they are less common. This is the area of phenomenon, which can include entities that don't belong, or ghosts etc. This is usually (though not always) found in older homes, ones which have been occupied by others and of which we may have little knowledge or history. This can also include merely past energies from previous occupants that have taken some time to emerge. Or it can be associated with traumatic deaths or happenings, or of messing with the occult, or of serious or misdirected drug use or of prolonger misery or illness. If the primary energy absorption consisted of positive and happy energies, there would be no "sense" or feeling that would lead us to consider a space clearing.

We hope to cover some aspects of these energies in this book, though it is a specialist area, and requires expert knowledge and handling. When called upon to perform this sort of work, I have always chosen to work alongside another professional, to ensure that "my back" is covered, so to speak. This way we can do the clearing effectively and then check on each other that we ourselves are totally free from picking up anything from the process that does not belong to us. Some entities can be more easily removed, but some stubborn ones really will need the assistance of a proven professional to clear.

Other or Less Common Energetic Problems

The aspect not always addressed comprehensively in the usual or more commonly available books or procedures of Space Clearing is the Fourth Stage I mention – Energetic Clearing; the Clearing of negative and unwanted energies and the Strengthening of the positive and nurturing Energies of a Space.

This is an extremely important aspect, particularly when there are shifts within the electro-magnetics of the Earth due to the recognized changes related to the Polar Magnetics that recently took place and continue to do so every ten to eleven years or so as a result of the Sun's regular electromagnetic shifts.

Feng Shui can go a long way to cover some of these aspects – things that can include places that house a lot of electrical appliances, positions of electricity meter boards, multiple computers and technical devices etc, but due to the continual earth changes, there is nothing wrong with regularly visiting these things to be sure that they are not affecting you or your personal energy systems or energy fields. Orgone devices can be very useful with electronic and electrical devices, assisting in keeping a healthy electromagnetic status.

What is Meant by Energetic Clearing?

Energetic Clearing does not necessarily mean that someone is performing a clearing in a very active or energetic manner (using a lot of energy or "elbow-grease") – it simply means that they are addressing a Space Clearing in a way that focuses on the unseen energy or energies involved.

Energy is all around us – it is everywhere. It is now scientifically proven that *everything* in our world is made up of energy. This includes not only the normal household electricity that we are aware of as a form of unseen energy, but also the foods that we eat which provides body energy. Even the chairs we sit on and the tables we eat at as well as we ourselves, our bodies and our thoughts are compromised of energy. We are made up of molecules and atoms vibrating and oscillating at their own appropriate speeds and frequencies.

Energy when referred to in Space Clearing can be described in many ways. It is sometimes what is "sensed" or felt as negative or uncomfortable, and it may sometimes be a feeling that is missing that should be there.

Usually positive energy simply feels good, welcoming, fresh, easy and "light".

To understand this concept further, and to keep this as simple as possible, think of a thought...

...if you were asked to think of something sad, then this would "color" your thoughts, and subsequently your energy systems.

[A Note here: If you have an understanding of the visible range of color that is observable to the human eye, and also the range of energies that is not visible to the human eye, yet still existing and quite real (and measurable by instrumentation), then you are beginning to understand the range of possibilities regarding color and frequencies. Each color has its own defining energy frequency and therefore its own individual vibration as demonstrated by scientific observations, monitors and measuring devices. Different colors; different energies; different emotions; different thoughts; they each have a different sense or feel about them. The range is huge, yet each is unique and has a different "sense", value, purpose or function.]

So back to the sad thought. Thinking about this long enough would cause your facial expression, posture and attitude to reflect the thought. You might well slouch, frown or find you have a "long face".

The same applies to happy or positive thoughts. Think of one for a moment – feel the difference in your body...

Happy thoughts often cause us to smile or appear chirpy. They can make our shoulders lighter and squarer, so to speak.

What is not commonly known, or immediately recognized is that -

Energy Always Follows Thought.

What do I mean by that, and why is it important?

And what does it have to do with a room or a space?

Let me explain...

This same sad thought, if thought of often enough, can become associated with the seat or space by the person thinking the thought, so that whenever that person sits in the same spot, he will very quickly if not immediately, go back to that particular thought (together with the associated feeling).

As he has been thinking the same thought, he has been adding energy to it, so that it is becoming stronger. This flows through into the energy space of that particular spot, and also to the furnishings or items closely contacted through this process. The same can be said for associating a certain spot with not just unhappy or negative thoughts but also positive ones such as thoughts of seeking a positive solution, and continually looking for the way to solve it.

Eventually, sitting in the same generally "positive" spot, the solution appears, and the means to do it.

To design or architect something, we first imagine or think the thought. Then we begin to design it in our mind. Eventually the thought becomes the building or project in actuality or physicality, unless we abort or abandon it ahead of time. For example: To complete a course of study demonstrates the ability of thought to manifest into reality. (Whereas indecisiveness shows the inability to manifest reality, or to get confused results.)

Consistent strong thoughts that are accompanied with emotion will imprint or "hang" in the atmosphere. A bit like the smog and smell of a certain kind of continual smoke. And the same is true of a very strong emotion.

People planning to do harm to others impact the atmosphere the same as those caring for and loving their families. You can almost tangibly feel when love is in the air.

What is not always realised, is that the energy that has surrounded the person thinking the sad thoughts in a particular seat often stays with the seat.

Psychics and clairvoyants can usually "read" the energies left behind on objects this way. Sensitive people can feel "yucky" when they pick up something that feels negative or doesn't feel "right" to them.

WHY DO SPACE CLEARING?

It should be coming obvious by now as to "Why?" one would do Space Clearing. We may get a sense that the space doesn't quite feel right. We may feel we need to reclaim our space. There can be a number of reasons why.

But the benefits may not always be so obvious.

When stuck, old, stale, negative, stagnant and dead energies are removed, and the area or space recharged, vitalized and replaced with fresh energies and become open to flow again, things can happen that couldn't happen before. And this is just from moving "stuck" energies. Imagine how the space would feel if old intense imprints and memories of anger, arguments, upsets, let-downs, pain or hurt were removed, so that the associated memories can be more easily forgotten and one can move on from unhappy recollections?

Apart from the above here are a few more suggestions as to Why one should do a Space Clearing, or at least be aware of what can happen in any space...

. A sense of unease in a certain corner or room

. Frequent Health problems which have arisen after shifting

. A drop in energy levels on entering the property or reluctance to spend time there

. The previous occupants suffered serious health problems, divorce or bankruptcy

. A difficult break up of a marriage or relationship

. A period of serious money worries

. Difficulty in selling your property

. Difficulties after moving into another property or premises

. Feeling worse after a healing or therapy session than one felt before the session

. Feeling sick or "off" when walking into or through a space or room

. Anytime you want to feel a "lift" in energy or mood

. Problems with concentrating, or a feeling that you are not alone or are being watched

. When the space suddenly feels very heavy, particularly after visitor/s

. Even though there are enough windows, the space still feels dark, or "heavy"

. Trouble sleeping, intrusive thoughts circling in one's mind, thoughts that you don't like and that you don't usually think

But what we haven't mentioned yet and what may begin to become obvious to you as WHY these problems exist in the first place.

And also HOW they are caused.

The Human Factor

Some of the most common reasons are simply because we are human.

Humans have emotions. Emotions are actually energy – the power of thought converted into motion within (internal focus) and without (external focus) the body.

Emotion can surround a person: I am sure that you will have been around someone at some time when they have exuded strong emotion, be it anger, excitement, fear, dread, passion or sadness. Each of us has our own energy field, and this has been visually and energetically recognized and photographed (Kirlian photography scientifically proved this many years ago) and the energetic frequency can now be measured by the latest sophisticated scientific equipment.

Our energy fields reflect what is happening in our emotions and our minds. Psychics can see and often "read" this. But not everyone can. Nevertheless, emotions, thoughts and feelings *are* there. And they can "rub-off" or affect other people's energy fields. And they can also rub off or "drop-off" onto furniture etc. Most of the time. this is all easily manageable – until you come to very intense energy. Unusual emotion or passion.

Powerful enough emotion or concentrated energy can not only impact on other people present in a room, but also impact on the space around an event. And this impact may last for a long time. This accounts for imprints made by events, and also by the fact that some psychics can accurately "read" these events. We are talking here about unusual events. But the gist of all this is that energy or emotion can leave an imprint, almost like a negative recording or snapshot, of an event, which can befuddle or confuse a space or place.

So in this case we may have occasion to use something a little stronger than just moving furniture around, vaccing up or spraying an environment. Emotions are not the only cause of energetic imprints. Thinking in itself can impact on a space. Clear thinking, arriving at positive solutions have a different effect on a space than negative, befuddled or chaotic thinking. It can almost be like the air itself gets tied up in knots and doesn't know how to sort itself out. Whereas clear thinking imprints can make us feel clear in the head. Both can create an energetic impact.

Benefits of Space Clearing

Increased productivity, harmony, peace or contentment are the usual and minimal expected results, sometimes and often coupled with better opportunities in many areas of life and work, as well as increased energy and verve for life.

For instance, to clear a bedroom properly will promote better and more restful quality sleep. This will impact on one's energy levels as well as one's resilience and attitude for the day. This increase in the sense of well-being will flow on to productivity and effectiveness in communication and relationships, assisting with the dynamics of relating, or career productivity. The sense of well being produced from restful sleep can promote health and success, and even support one's love life.

That was just doing the bedroom!

So how about looking into the other rooms of the house? What would happen if shared common areas are improved? If living in a flat where energies can be absorbed into your room from below (or above) are arrested and no longer affect the functioning of your own life. If energetic toxicity or interference ceases and no longer affects you?

Surely it's worth checking these out? So I hope I have given you sufficient reason and inspiration to explore how you can enhance and improve your living and working places.

What Needs Space Clearing?

Any and every space benefits from a regular "clearing", but in particular it is an essential practice for any place that feels "dark", "heavy", cluttered, "not comfortable", uninviting or unfriendly, or is overloaded with a sense or "presence" of another whether living or dead, or that doesn't allow for a feeling of expansion that is not related to size, or that doesn't provide a sense of welcome, nurturing or comfort.

Areas that get a lot of focused concentration can accumulate dead thought energy, particularly when related to unsolved issues or problems. Stagnant energies can build up and disrupt the flow of energy in a space or place. .

Other areas that need clearing are: Places that have experienced traumatic events, prolonged unhappy periods, lengthy sickness or disease, lots of clutter or lack of caring attention. Places that make one feel intimidated, or that carry unpleasant or painful memories that overwhelm any current pleasant happenings.

A jail will immediately bring to mind the sort of thing I mean, though this may seem to be an exaggerated example. However, I do know of places that made me feel really uncomfortable – one empty house I was looking at buying many years ago gave me the "willies" until I discovered the horrific past experience it still retained.

Being as sensitive as I am, I practically ran out the place despite my "brave" attempts to check it out. Upon further insistent questioning, the estate agent admitted that the place had not only been a brothel, but boasted a murder within its walls. Phoooh! Glad I was out of there... Now I always listen to my instinct about such things.

Other places can be work situations. Gossip can build-up as well as rivalry, resentments, petty jealousies and little nasty-nesses that can interfere with one's productivity. Personal competitive attacks can impact on the space, as well as those unseen issues of unresolved tensions from the home front that are brought into the work place by oneself or others.

Even some hotel rooms may need a "mini-clearing" as they can carry the marks of the previous renting occupier or occupiers, though fortunately, due to the transient nature of these rooms, they are generally more likely to contain "jumbled" or erratic energies rather than fearful.

Conversely, you may notice the sense of ease and welcome in some Bed and Breakfast places, or Boutique Hotels, where you can feel the caring or welcome of the owners who have a personal interest in your comfort and well-being. Some are able to suffuse this positive energy into the atmosphere and the furnishings, as well as even the food.

Some cars need Space Clearing too, particularly if second hand. If you have loaned your vehicle out, or just had it serviced, the sensitive amongst you will feel the initial subtle difference when you first get back into your car. Caravans can be included here. Easy to fix, you need just a little care and knowledge, and you can clear past owner impacts.

And of course, I find that when workmen have been to repair or fix something, that I have to clear their energies from the space again. Not that they are "bad" people, not at all, but they can bring their own problems or attitudes into the space. If they drink a lot or take drugs, they may introduce this energy into one's home space, and the sensitive type of person will feel it in some way.

As I see clients in my home clinic as well as professional rooms, clearing and protecting the working space after treatments is all part of my normal space maintenance, and so I extend it to any living areas if any trades-people have been.

It is also noteworthy too, that when someone walks or works in a "clear" space, then their energy bodies relax, especially when they are not used to feeling so safe, and they quite literally "drop" their energetic residues into the space. This needs to be cleared up or it can affect the client immediately following them.

Paying attention to maintain the space is so necessary. As well as taking care with whom you invite into your home space if they are a stranger.

For those of you who work from home, be it as writer, artist, IT professional, consultant etc, maintaining your own space after certain visitors or uninvited others have been in and "disturbed" your "vibes" can be an important consideration, so it is remember after clearing your space to reintroduce your own vibes back into it again consciously.

WHEN TO DO SPACE CLEARING

In case you are still in any doubt as to when it is an appropriate time to do Space Clearing, and you jump straight to this section, I have put some ideas down here for you.

For me, the moment I feel uncomfortable or sense intrusive energies, I will immediately check in with my knowing to ascertain what has changed or affected the space. The tools later listed are an easy check to see what is required or appropriate to resolve the issue and to effect a clearing as soon as possible.

One can do a mini Space Clearing any time, particularly if you have done a proper Space Clearing previously, and some occurrence has muddied up the space again. We cannot live in an inter-action free world, and things do happen, but when we are confident that what comes into our homes in the form of unwanted or negative attentions or energies, can also be taken out of our homes safely and relatively easily, then it gives us pleasure and confidence in the fact that we have some measure of control over our own special and intimate environment.

Our home, after all, is where we go to for rest and recuperation, for familiarity, to relax and simply "be" as well as "do" the things we like to for ourselves (and our families if we have one).

I would suggest that after reading this book, if you haven't already done so, that you perform a full basic Space Clearing as soon as you can, and note the feeling and ambience of the space both before your clearing and afterwards.

This then will become your guide and barometer for future Space Clearings, be they a comprehensive one or a mini treatment.

Reasons to consider doing any sort of Space Clearing:

. When the space suddenly feels heavy, particularly after visitor/s

. When you wake up and feel a bit "under the weather" for no real reason

. When you feel it needs to be done

. When you have the time to cover the main basic points of a Space Clearing

. When you have done your weekly or regular clean up of the house or property (this may be your declutter step)

. Before you are holding a special meeting, or celebration or you are wanting to set a special or sanctified space

. Directly after you have had a group of people in your home or place and you feel the need to reclaim your space

. Anytime you want to feel a "lift" in energy or mood {Check out the "Quick Solutions" for a quick treatment

. And any other reason in "Why do Space Clearing"

The "How" - Space Clearing Techniques

This book deals with physical, energetic, mental, emotional, spiritual and psychic energy clearings.

We will define the spaces to be cleared and then the appropriate methods, treatment or approach for each of them. You are welcome to combine any approaches if that is what feels right to you. However, to be thorough, it may also be wise to consider all of the elements of these methods before omitting any steps, whether you add something else or not.

Remember to prepare yourself before beginning the clearing, for best and safest results.

Here is the order that I have found works best for thorough or comprehensive Space Clearing

.Assess the space

> Define the Problem
>
> Define the Space
>
> Define the Boundaries

.Prepare Yourself and Your "Tools"

.De-clutter Items and Objects if possible beforehand

.Work Methodically, to a List or Define what Steps you will take before you begin

.End the Clearing Session when the space feels clear

.Clean Yourself Up (again) After

Define the Problem/s

If possible, move from the assessment of "not-quite-right" or "needs something" to get clearer on what could be required. Consider the following to get a better idea. They may apply to physical things and placements as well as visual or energetic problems. Ask yourself is any of the following are part of the problem.

.Lack of Space or Room for movement – Feng Shui?

.Stagnant Energies / Lack of Vitality

.Inharmonious Atmosphere

.Negative Energies

.Energy Disturbances: Arguments, Disruption, Violence

."Heavy" or Confusing Energies or Invasive Energies from Another Person or Presence

.Grief or "Loss" or other downer Energies

.Spots that always feel "sad" or hold painful memories

.Uncomfortable or "cold" areas

Define the Space

. The Home, House, Unit or Dwelling

. Work Space, Office, Work Station

. Garden

. Motor Car or Transport Vehicle

. Caravan etc

The Process And Intention Of Space Clearing

Obviously the initial intention is to "feel better" in a certain space or place.

We recognize change on a physical level straight away. You can always tell when a place has been cleared, tidied, washed, dusted, swept and polished.

Your intention when performing Space Clearing is initially to cleanse the space from anything that is toxic, interfering, stagnating, negative, inharmonious, erratic, chaotic, confusing or dirty in an energetic or "sense" / feeling way.

The problem of course, that this stuff is not always visible or identifiable. That's where we have to learn to be smart about it, or at the very least, thorough!

That means being aware of the possibilities, and covering your bases.

Sensitive people will often get this quicker, but the less sensitive can still work this out for themselves, when they figure out the right questions to ask.

The quality of your question will decide or dictate the quality of the answer. And questions will be included later on.

So view your task with the intention of sorting out Energy: Tidy, organise, empty, create order, un-clutter, arrange, neaten, make clean or transparent, free from imprints, toxic interference, or any other devices: by the intention of your mind, and by asking the right question, together with the right intent and statement.

Visualisation — Free, Easy, Repeatable

A powerful tool to use it to work with your Higher Self and the support provided by the higher energies – you may perceive them to be known to you as any of the following:

God, Infinite Spirit, Divine Source, The All-That-Is, Mother-Father-God, The God/Goddess, or some other title that means the highest and purest and best source of light, love and energy that you are aware of.

Some people like or prefer to work with what they refer to as their Guides, or with the Angelic Realm. Whatever is the highest and most powerful in a safe and loving way, this is what you are aiming to contact and connect with in order to do the unseen energy work.

There is a difference between being Psychic and being Spiritual.

Though I have known many spiritual people, they were not always psychic in the accepted sense of the word, psychic generally meaning the following: clairvoyant (seeing things beyond normal vision), clairsentient (feeling or sensing things beyond normal sensing), clairaudient (hearing things not of normal speech or sound). But they have had a comprehension of the spiritual aspects of life, and I do not mean those things covered by the "spiritualist" or "spiritist" as these often deal with psychic phenomena and mediumship. Which are not necessarily about true spirituality.

Psychic and spiritual are not both about the same thing. It is interesting to note that when using the same technique, a psychic and someone spiritual may achieve different results because of where their consciousness lies.

Visualisation is a tool that can be used by anyone, not just the Psychic and the Spiritual. If you are already psychic, putting aside issues of power, force, ego, will bring you better results in Space Clearing.

The truth is that we are all spiritual beings, though some to a greater or lesser degree – what is meant here is that each of us is a being of spirit living within a physical body, and as such we have the ability to be in contact with this inner spirit, which is by its nature part of the "God-force" or "Divine Source". So working consciously for the will of the highest "God" or "Divine Source" to work through us will bring better results to any energy work that we undertake.

You can of course combine both psychic skills and spiritual aspects together, and this can bring great results, as the spiritual aspects will override any personal power or ego agendas.

One of the great tools for energy work is the Visualisation skill – which needs to work consciously with knowledge and appropriateness to achieve the best results. Visualising by itself can achieve a certain amount, but when coupled with not only spirituality, and also knowledge on energy, vibrations, colors and sounds, then one can create profound changes and enhancements to a space.

Even though I was sensitive and spiritual, and had the "right" intention to clean and clear a space, when I learned about the combinations of color, form, application and function, then I was really able to do it well, and in safety.

In this book I present the techniques that I have worked with for many years that have proven themselves over and over.

Places And Spaces

"New" Home Layers

A word here on living in a new home (new to you, that is) – the initial Space Clearing will make a big difference to the feel and energy of a residence. But over time and as you continue to live in your "new" place, your personal energies can cause the deeper layers of old imprints to continue to emerge. I have seen this happen several times – and it is not to do with a faulty Space Clearing. This is just the nature of old and impacted energies. They emerge when the upper layers are freed up and gone – they ooze out, so to speak, as the new (different? happier?) energies begin to penetrate and they create a dis-resonance with what has gone before.

A friend of mine who is an excellent psychic did a full clearing on her home. For several weeks everyone was quite content and happy. Then she started waking up feeling tired and depressed, and felt that she just couldn't get her act together.

After a few days of crawling back to bed, she talked to me about it. Between the two of us, we came to recognize this was simply more of the previous owners past history and struggle with ill-health emerging from the space, ethers, and indeed from underneath the house, where several other layers were now emerging.

These were cleared between us very quickly, and after the last release took place about six months later, there were no more problems in the space, and indeed the house now felt like it was "hers" and supporting her again.

Geographic Relocation

When you relocate into another place or area, you enter a different space, one which has not yet known your energies. Even if you have built a new home, the space will hold the frequencies of the workers and builders as well as the frequencies of the land you built upon and its previous residents or landowners. Not every place is initially welcoming or harmonious, and the dis-resonance can be felt.

It is important then to clear the space from previous occupiers in whatever form, as well as align yourself to the new energy you will be living in.

In Australia there is often a ready recognition of the original tribal Guardians of the land, and often those that are aware will request permission from the Guardian to live there peacefully. This is done in appreciation and with respect and does not necessarily need a formal ritual, but is more of a heart thing. I have felt these "elders" or guardians myself. And when I visited England I felt the more recently and current "imported Guardians" that had been brought over by other nationalities, tribes, religions and races, and these felt like they were clamouring and arguing for territory with the existing resident guardians. This created a lot of unrest in certain areas.

Whatever new geo-location you find yourself in, simply acknowledging the intelligence of the place and stating that you come in peace will create a good basis for peaceful co-existence. If you are of sensitive nature and feel any initial resistance, simply continue to reiterate that you mean now harm with respect until they stop their grumbling and have completed their looking-you-over. (This was once my experience and it worked.) Some residential problems can come from this lack of respect and recognition for previous ownership.

This is not to say that you have no power or control over a place, for you are your own sovereign. However, when it comes to space clearing if there is a history from previous occupiers, tribes, races or land-owners that have brought a forceful or argumentative or disrespectful energy, this can affect a property.

I have only ever heard one story of a person having to leave again because they had serious problems with the land Guardian which couldn't be sorted out this way.

It is also an interesting and sometimes necessary exercise when leaving any place to give thanks, and to ensure that you have withdrawn all of your own personal energies from that place safely in order for you to re-anchor yourself again in your new abode.

There is also suggested remedy of verbal intent included in the Statements section under "Affirmations to Clear".

Aligning to Your Home's Energy

This aspect is missed by many doing house clearings on a pre-owned home. Yet it is such a vitally important one.

Not only must the residence align to us, but we must consider how we can align to the home!

When a home is dreamed up, thought of, designed and planned, it is like it gains some kind of identity as to its purpose. For instance, a hotel is designed to cater for certain appetites or needs, a health spa is generally designed and intended to assist with health and a factory is intended to make money and provide space for enterprise. Generally speaking.

When a building conversion takes place, the original purpose or mission if you like, is still part of the building and its identity. Consider a brothel, and then the attempt to convert it to a family home... For the sensitive, the very idea feels weird and somewhat uncomfortable.

So when a building has been erected purely to make money, to profit from the activity of building for rent or to onsell for profit, etc, it may take quite a lot of time for it to build a heart, so to speak. And it just may never get there, for its intention is not to nurture family and relationships, but to nurture making money. So whilst the careers of residents may be furthered, happy relating might not get the same support from the place being lived in.

An interesting concept, yes, but for some people it really does affect how they function in the home.

And a residence just might get a history of failed relationships, because it absorbs the energy of one divorce and may even imbue this energy into the next relationship that tries to create its nest there.

Whilst homes that were designed to fulfill and nurture family members and bring harmony and a long and happy marriage, can often assist in achieving just that. And some of these homes or buildings can get a reputation for being happy place to live.

So, if this appears relevant in your house clearing, it is important to attempt to understand the initial purpose of your building in order to align with it, and to add to its purpose to better further your relationship with it. A kind of working-with-your-home to achieve a joint beneficial long term outcome.

Everything that exists has its own thoughtform, its own intended purpose, attached to it on an unseen level. Those that have psychic vision can often pick up on the original thoughtform or design of the place, and be able to ask the intent of the house to work together with the occupants.

Not only those who can see clairvoyantly, but if you yourself personally take the time to listen, or to feel and enquire of the space you are in, you may well get the gist of its original intent and purpose. Then you have a basis on which to begin to join forces, so to speak, in order for you to be happy there, and for the house to be happy that you are there. Some may find this idea too much to embrace, but speaking from a metaphysical and energetic point of view, this mutual cooperation can save much heartache.

For with everything created, there is first an intent, an imagining, a given purpose, and it is designed accordingly. And then it is manifested materially until it is no longer just a thought, just a blueprint, just a design – it becomes a physical construction, complete with its intended purpose.

You cannot make a train turn into a boat, you cannot make a kennel become a mansion. But given certain individual limitations and working with these and within these, you can re-purpose something to be of benefit.

Alignment

This requires the ability to be honest with yourself, and to be able to listen to others, for that is the basis of simple negotiation called for on a heart level and a consciousness level here.

To align yourself to your "new" home, first acknowledge its past history (whatever it is), then see if you can identify its original purpose, see if you can harmoniously harness this to work for your intended use of the place, and see if this is acceptable to the property. If it's not, try renegotiating until what you come up with is acceptable, or you will always have conflict present at some deep level, which may affect all you do.

When you find the acceptable goals and purpose, make an internal agreement (you can also verbalise this in your own way) with the property, keeping in mind gratitude for what the property can bring to this new joint venture, and allow this to be set as your intent too. And keep to it!

Congratulations! You have connected to the heart of your home!

Work Place Issues

When working with others in an office situation the ideal environment is one that gives us our own private work space, complete with clear physical boundaries such as walls, windows and doors. It is easier to maintain personal boundaries when we have physical ones. However this is not always possible. And many offices have shared spaces or even open areas.

When there is little physical protection from the obvious intrusions of others, for sensitive types it can become a priority that they know how to protect their own energetic boundaries and energy fields more so than the average person.

It is suggested that you treat the area you work in similarly as to how you clear your personal living space, and that you begin by getting clear on the area you occupy and therefore have a right to clear for yourself. As in house clearing, first delineate your area by your painting the whole of the space that is your personal working space, using the Gold paint to assist in setting up clear boundaries. Then proceed as you would for your home.

Add personal items to individualise, beautify, territorise or otherwise show this is clearly your space without it contradicting its original purpose of business or service. This helps to bring in your own personal energy and reminds others of this in a kindly way.

Use a mirror if your back faces a door or an open space. Pot plants help bring some freshness and can help with cleansing the air. Some people use protecting or grounding crystals that look like ornaments.

Work on strengthening your Energy Fields will also support you.

Vehicles

Use the same methods here on your vehicle.

Oftentimes a good wash / mopping and vacuuming can sort and clear many things, but after repairs, servicing, impacts, or someone else using it, you can use the same space clearing methods to claim your vehicle as your own space again. Paint as previously instructed to clean and clear.

Having said this, I would also like to add that you can further extend a form of energy protection to your vehicle as you travel.

I practice energetic protection on myself, as I am quite sensitive, and I extend my energetic protection to my car. This usually means that I remind myself when driving that the car is now my container and the current boundary to my energy fields, and that my car prevents other's unwanted energies from coming into my car. It's like a kind of two-way boundary that keeps my inner car space clear.

It is no use me cleaning and clearing my home only to bring back home somebody's angry tantrums that have gotten into my car simply by me driving next or past them.

I also extend protection when I park my car, asking that it is invisible to problem seekers or intruders. Just an added precaution.

Hospitals / Waiting Rooms

Even though a hospital room is not space that you personally own or pay rent for, because it is prone to the energies of others, I do not hesitate to do clearings of the space for an injured or ill friend or family member. When emergency situations call for prolonged hospitalization, there is sometimes a need to understand the energy dynamics for those involved, be it patient, family of patient, visitors or even staff members.

If you have a child who is hospitalized, you may create a circle around their bed and space, or room if they have one.

Paint this with Gold as instructed and periodically check if further attention is required for anything else. Space sprays can be very supportive to help refresh the patient and their space. You do not need to un-Paint the walls or space, and it may possibly benefit anyone else using the same space – at least for a while.

The Complete Space Clearing Process

Preparation For Clearing

Familiarize yourself if possible with how to use a pendulum, as you can use this to assess the energy status of a room. Instructions are provided.

To achieve the best results, it is important that you prepare ahead, and assemble necessary tools as much as possible.

When you have de-cluttered or tidied up, you may find that you immediately want to vacuum up or sweep up, etc. Do it. This helps you feel that the space is cleaned (in the normal sense of the word) and gives you a good basis to continue with the Space Clearing.

The next step and the most important step, whether you declutter first or later is this:

Prepare Yourself!

Having assessed the energy status of the room, and allowed for sufficient time to complete your task, start off wherever possible with a shower or bath. Prepare yourself mentally and energetically whilst you are showering. That means move into the frame of mind of what you will be doing and your objective. If you consciously work with Guidance, you can begin to call them in to assist you. If you believe in God / The-All-That-Is, you can start your inner prayers or invocations for the highest and best outcome, and for protection as you cleanse.

Aligning with your Higher Self can be a powerful way to align to your Clearing intents and abilities.

I usually light a candle at the beginning of the Space Clearing.

Assemble Your Tools!

This simply means have ready or to hand the tools you think you may need during this process. I have listed the items I keep in my Space Clearing Kit...

Space Clearing Kits

EVERYONE serious about Space Clearing should have an "Energy Clearing Kit", and I have listed the basic items below. Following the list you will find detailed information as to their function, use and benefit.

This is by no means definitive, but is a really good basic kit that should cover almost all problems likely to be encountered by the average person.

In the Optional Extras are some items that can be useful for work situations or other situations outside of the home.

. Candles

. Brass Tibetan Bowl / Cymbals or other Music / Sound / Mantra

. Sage / Smudge Stick or Incense / Essential Oils

. Spray for Space / Hair

. Brass Burning Bowl etc if doing a Burn-off

. Bucket (Imaginary)

. Script / Wordage / Knowledge

. Intent & Visualisation (Room by Room work)

FULL SPACE CLEARING TREATMENT

If you are performing a space clearing for the first time in your home, this is the full list and order that experience has shown to work the best. You may not need all points, but you can use this as a handy guide.

. House clean and vacuum up beforehand

. Declutter if necessary

. Self preparation – wash or bath. Prepare mentally and energetically.

. Align with your inner essence /Higher Self / Guides or your Divine Source / God etc.

. Light one or more candles

. Assess the energy status of the room

. Assess what you need to clear – have Scripts ready to help

. Prepare Burn-off Brass Bowl

. If desired or required, play Durga Mantra or other music – Use sound to clear and move energy

. You can simultaneously use incense, oils or smudge stick, room by room

. Paint as per instructions under Tools – Room by Room

. Check the space again, to see if whatever it was has shifted

. Repeat the process until the space feels right to you, and you feel you can relax in it again

. (If you know the source of the problem (arguments etc) then you have a guide to work with already)

. (If you know how to muscle test (see my easy Kinesiology self-test tool in *Secrets Behind Energy*

Fields") or pendulum then you can scan the list quickly to find the best priority solution)

. Finish the space clearing with a burning-off if you didn't do one during the process

. Infill the space with treatments, soothing music, flowers, re-check placements of objects

. Wash and clean up, change clothing

. Enjoy!

QUICK MINI CLEARING

When you have done proper Space Clearings but something happens that needs a quick fix or immediate attention, then you can use these suggestions.

Though I give instructions regarding preparing and having a bath, if speed is of the essence then you can quickly wash your hands and arms to your elbows, cleanse, wash or wipe your face, and wash or wipe your neck (especially at the back where we often pick up negative energy). Instead of washing your hair (which collects dross and residual energies) you can spray through your hair (lifting it up and shaking it through and out) with an essential oil or something that you feel will clean out any energetic crap you have picked up, or if you have really short hair, run a wet facecloth or some water over it to "rinse" it energetically.

Remember that thought and intent at the same time really helps move stuff off quickly. You can use your pendulum to identify which of the steps below otherwise go through them all. (If you know how to muscle test you can use that tool to scan the list quickly to find the best priority solutions.

. Quick cleanse of self as just suggested above

. If you know how to, then align with your inner essence or your Guides or your Divine Source / God etc.

. Assess the energy status of the room and what you think you need to clear

. Recheck the Painted walls and repair if necessary

. Go through your Tools Kit or the Tools List I have provided, and check in with yourself to see what feels or seems appropriate. You can use your pendulum to see what tool is indicated

. Check the space again, to see if whatever it was has shifted

. Repeat process until the space feels right to you, or your pendulum happily swings clockwise in a circular motion and you feel you can relax again

Essential Aids To Clearing

Pendulum

Using a pendulum is such a simple yet powerful technique that I include instructions here for those who are not familiar with them.

In Space Clearing I usually combine kinesiology, using a Pendulum and a pre-set idea of the tools that I think I may need. Even though I am quite sensitive, I often count on the visual actions of pendulum testing to ensure and establish a visual reading of the state of the energy of a room, as well as my own energetic reading using my own self testing finger indicator test (kinesiology self-test).

(Kinesiology is another form of gaining information via a feedback system – in these situations I use it in a simplified finger test.)

Asking the pendulum to **"Show me now what this room / space is doing"** can reveal its energetic capability in the form of a visual arc and direction of motion as well as speed of motion.

A sludgy type of action from the pendulum can indicate toxicity or tiredness, or a build-up of negativity. Whilst a smooth and quickening circular spiral can indicate a clear space. At the very least there should be a clear difference with the same test at the end of the Space Clearing. Again, I find it more beneficial to use as many tools as I have available to ensure that I cover all of the bases.

I now know that when a room is in good condition and that there are no current energetic distractions in the space, no imprints to be moved on or out, no unseen toxicities or negative energies, that my pendulum will indicate this with a clear clockwise circular motion –

indicating that current frequencies show a positive vortex action and that the room is energised again. This testing tool allows me to ensure that I continue clearing a room until I get this clear indication. Rather than simply guessing that I have cleared it.

How to Use a Pendulum

The secret to using a pendulum is to let it respond to the energy available and to discover what constitutes an affirmative indication (a "Yes") or a negative indication (a "No").

A pendulum is a mechanism that shows energy movement clearly by rotation or movement via a suspended crystal or weight at the end of a chain or cord. There are many types available in shops and you should be able to find one that feels right for you. Or you can simply make your own. The weight should not be too heavy, nor too light.

You can test it is responding by asking the pendulum to show you what a "Yes" is and what a "No" is. This is best done by resting your arm or elbow on a stable surface so as to minimise any interference from you or others that will prevent it from swinging freely and autonomously. (Be patient if you find you are a bit unsure to begin with, let yourself play with it a little. You will eventually get more comfortable with it.)

It will guide itself, and you may well find some pendulums respond better and more freely to your instruction than others. Choose from one of these when selecting one.

If you do not get any response at all, either you are not clear enough with your intent or the pendulum is unable to read energy and respond to it. Crystal pendants are usually more reliable in providing feedback in this way than other substances.

I have also taken to attaching my pendulum to another longer horizontal crystal wand so that when I work with it, my fingers are not touching it, and it is suspended from the middle of the longer crystal. You could use a piece of wood or anything else that creates a fulcrum effect if you wish.

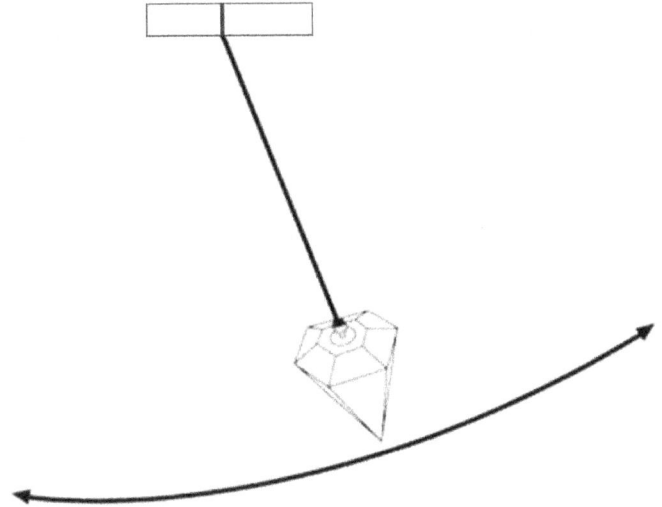

**Pendulum may swing in a forward—backward motion
Or side to side motion**

Pendulum movements are generally:

- straight line - side to side or front and back
- circles - clockwise or counterclockwise
- elliptical motion

- some pendulums bob up and down to indicate strong action, usually affirmative

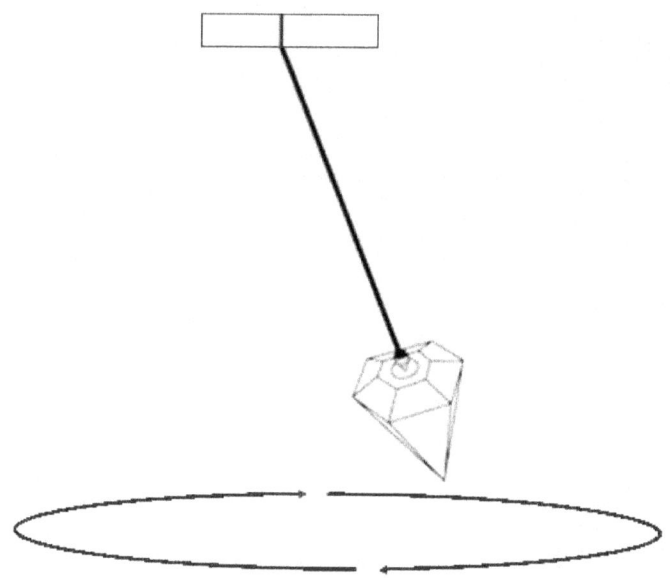

Pendulum may swing in a circular motion

When seeking an indication from the pendulum you must determine the direction your pendulum will take for Yes and for No.

Hold the pendulum in your stabilised hand. With the other hand - touch the point to steady its motion.

Keep your eyes on the point.

Now address the pendulum and say, "Show me 'Yes'." It will soon swing in one direction, which could be side to side, back and forth, or circles.

Now say, "Show me No." It should swing in the opposite direction.

Be certain the pendulum is not being guided by the movement of your hand or fingers.

Once you have determined the pattern for Yes and No - you are ready to begin.

Generally, the faster the movement - the stronger the energies.

Testing the Space

Now you can hold or position the crystal pendulum in the centre of the space you are working in and ask it to *"Show me what this room is doing"*. The pendulum will respond and indicate what is happening. This action can be performed before clearing a space, and afterwards to provide you with comparisons.

DE-CLUTTER
What it is and How to Do It

Most of us in some form or another are able to keep on top of too much accumulation of trash or rubbish in our homes and environment. Generally. Most of us clear our space on this level regularly. Even so, there are times when we sometimes can suddenly realize that we have been too busy to do more than just a quick or regular clean and tidy. When doing a culling or clearing of personal objects, furnishings or possessions, you can rate what needs to be sorted according to your own levels of comfort.

De-Clutter simply means to remove existing clutter to create a more tidy and current environment.

A Declutter of a space is also invaluable when there has been neglect of some kind, or a major trauma that has prevented regular upkeep, clearing or maintenance, and things may have gotten out of hand.

In this book the basics of decluttering are outlined for when you find that you have some serious stuff to clear out, or if you feel you really need to do some sort of reorganizing or rearranging together with your Space Clearing.

The Declutter process can be skipped, if your place doesn't need it. However, for most people the accumulations can be responsible for the stuck or stagnant energies, and this process can get the energies moving again. There is no rule about all of this, just suggestions as to what you can do to improve the energy flow in your environment. Most people always feel better when "stuff" has been gotten rid of or put away tidily *where it belongs*. So choose those steps which feel right to you or suit what you can accomplish.

You can achieve a lot simply by cleaning out what is broken, outworn, no longer needed, no longer brings you ease or enjoyment, or what no longer feels "right". It can be a professional business in itself, as some people have such trouble throwing old stuff away.

There is much you can do yourself without having to go to this length, but if you need it, help is there. And it will go through everything in your home and life: furniture, clothing, paperwork, bathroom medicine and makeup chests, kitchen gadgetry etc.

When it comes right down to it, to actually letting go, a prime consideration can be:

Whatever makes you happy, whatever you love, whatever you use – these are the things to cherish. And hold onto for longer.

Nothing ever stays the same, nothing is guaranteed, nothing ever goes with us when we die, we come into this life with nothing and leave the same way, so nothing truly "belongs" to us – we can never really "own" or possess anything.

Most of the things we possess in life are really only on loan to us, for they stay when we have gone. Learning the lesson of detachment can help us to live in the flow of life, secure that whatever the situation, our needs will always be provided for us.

Do It Yourself Declutter

To do it by yourself, and to make it simple, sort into piles, starting and finishing a room at time. You may find that it can improve your space tremendously, and also give you a little more work to do when you discover some things left undone. It may be wise to continue to focus on the Space Clearing and make dates to complete any tasks or business arising from your de-clutter exercise.

Begin by sorting things into separate piles – for instance you can have piles like this:

- What I want to keep
- What I want to get rid of
- What I am not sure about

You may then expand on these piles, especially the "keep" pile:

- What I use daily and need to be able to get at quickly and easily
- What I use regularly or weekly
- What I use seasonally and can store out of sight or elsewhere
- What is current

The "Get Rid of" pile may be further sorted like this:

- What I want to throw away right now
- What I can give away to friends or relatives right now because I know I no longer need it/ it no longer fits / it is no longer of use to me but is good enough to give to someone else I know
- What I can pass on to charities
- What I can sell or share at a garage sale

The "What I am not sure about" pile can be rethought of as:

> . What I am not sure about and need to think about for a month
>
> . What I am not sure about and need to see if I use next season / year / next semester

Or you may be brave enough to make decisions after having another sort through in a couple of weeks or so...

Of course, the above is just a general guide, and you will need to vary your approach depending on the room you are working with.

For instance, in the kitchen you will be checking use-by-dates, and throwing outdated stuff out. You may find you have a double up on certain herbs, so you will be putting them into appropriate containers or labeling containers or relabeling etc. And also placing herbs in the order of most use being the easiest to get at. See the section on Feng Shui for further ideas.

In the tool shed (or even the kitchen or bathroom), you can consider putting up shelves for ease of access or for increased storage space. Or putting up hooks for pans, utensils, tools or gadgets.

Once you set your mind to looking for storage and access solutions, you may be surprised at the answers you get. The myriad types and sizes in glass, cardboard, wood, plastic or cane containers makes attractive storage easier.

What you may also find when coming to domestic papers is that tidying and decluttering old newspapers or brochures or going through old paperwork may actually remind you of things left undone, which may give you a pile you label:

> . What do I want to action soon or now

. What do I want to keep as future reference

So, I would suggest that you continue focusing on your declutter, and when you have finished, you can sort these into the appropriate piles that mean something to you, and set dates when you want to look at them and work on them. This way you won't get too sidetracked and find yourself bogged down under a ton of clothes and paperwork, feeling more pressured than before.

So remember, sort first, get rid of what you can, and for the rest, allocate set times to deal with what comes out of your clearing.

Before getting on with your Space Clearing take a moment to read this first...

Finish off your Declutter

...to Suit *You*

Don't get too hung up on the declutter section – don't get hung up on the lack of your time right now to sort through everything - don't let it stop you from doing an energetic clearing if you feel it is necessary and you don't have enough time to go through and sort or tidy up absolutely everything that needs going through.

If you are challenged this way and are short of the time required to thoroughly go through all your paperwork or clear your cupboards, then do it in stages. Decide what you can handle now, and simply box what still needs to be gone through and move it out (and store it in a place that you are yet to clear i.e. cellar or attic or spare room) or allocate another time to do it properly.

And you can always build the rest of the decluttering into your weekly or regular domestic house cleaning. Include some aspect of decluttering into your domestic chores until you have finished, then it is a simple matter to declutter as you go, so to speak. Or at the very least, when next you need to sort out accumulations again, there will be less to have to sort through.

Most people do a regular clean and / or tidy. Most people do not realize that doing the laundry is an act of cleansing and clearing of energies. As is sweeping and mopping up, and of vacuuming up. It may be a somewhat limited energetic clearing, but it is definitely a clearing, especially when disposing of the debris vacced up.

Ensure that piles of dirt are removed if sweeping up, and that the vacuum bag is emptied regularly. To see how powerful simply vaccing up is, read the section on "Vacuuming & Sweeping".

At this point, performing some Feng Shui type techniques will also add a further dimension to your declutter, bearing in mind not to "fill" the spaces again too readily, thus allowing for a better flow of energy to move and sustain our defined area.

FENG SHUI

Here are some suggestions and ideas for applying Feng Shui techniques to any space or place. Feng Shui is of course, a complete philosophy and application in itself, and this book does not intend to replace this modality completely. However, there are many varied applications of Feng Shui, each of them valid, and they range from the astrology of the person who owns a building or space, through the geolocation and position of a building or particular room, through to the design, style and colour application within a given space.

Bear in mind that the real meaning and purpose of Feng Shui is in the managing and governing of energy flow into and through a space. If there is no room for flow, then there is clutter and eventually stagnation. This then prevents movement towards one's goals, and an allowing for good or better things to occupy the same space.

Directing energy movement doesn't need to be difficult. An awareness of when something doesn't quite feel right, or feels difficult or uncomfortable to navigate through is a good intuitive indicator that something needs to be placed differently, or be removed, or be revamped.

Of course, not everyone has the time to devote to a full Feng Shui, nor even the money to throw out what they possess in order to replace it with more "Zen" like or aesthetically pleasing furniture, so finding solutions that fit your budget and that please you personally is generally the best way to go.

Here are some general ideas to guide you in your own Feng Shui type enhancements.

DIY Feng Shui

Arrangement of Furniture can Enhance your Room's Décor

Arranging current furniture in the right manner can ensure that a room area is more efficiently used and more pleasing to the eye. A clever furniture arrangement can also highlight a favourite piece of furniture. However, figuring out the best way to utilize space and create a comfortable atmosphere can be a difficult chore. But with some planning and creativity, it can be accomplished easier than you think.

Before you move anything, it's best to decide what the focal point of the room or space is going to be. Each room has a purpose, and some of use a room for several purposes; lounge rooms can be used not just for "lounging" and reading, watching TV, but also for entertaining, playing or working on a computer (if one doesn't have separate rooms for any of these other activities) or an artistic hobby. Where the TV is present, most people make this the focal point, whilst other focus on the coffee table or centre of the room. It is all purely a personal point.

Take a moment to focus your effort around imagining what is important to accomplish or perform in this room and try out various placements. I find it helps to get several pieces of paper and do a rough drawing of the placement of furniture. I start off with an existing diagram, then I see if I can re-position them better. Part of this re-arranging of furniture in a room is to decide on what you need to be easily accessible, and imagine how you can make that work with your given furniture and the positions of the doors and windows.

You can also focus or centre your furniture arrangement around a particular focal point as already mentioned, and it can be anything; a fireplace, a picture window, a table and centre-piece, a view, a home entertainment center or a wall painting.

When positioning chairs, armchairs or couches try to place them within about eight feet of each other to encourage conversation. Position a table in such a way that it is easily accessible from every chair where possible, or if you are constrained with space, place one chair between the table and the wall to allow more movement around the other sides of the table when all chairs are not in use. Try to keep a light source near the seating area. Coffee tables are often best to have a clearance of about 14 to 18 inches from the sofa to allow legs and knees bruise-less access and easy reach for the placement of cups or glasses etc. if you have Side Tables, these could be at least as tall as the arm of the chairs or sofa to make serving easy and discourage accidental spills. When arranging furniture, make sure you provide enough space to move around the room.

And this is the key to energy movement. If you could imagine a swirl of coloured wind or smoke (only imaginary!) gently blowing into a room through its door (and any other access points) and there is no room for it to flow-by-and-past items of furniture, then you can see what things will block energy. This needs to be balanced, obviously, and is only a visual guide, as we sometimes need some things to stop energy or to be the focus of it – such as the back of a bookcase or lounge couch in a large space, which serves as a zoning mechanism or a room divider.

In a multipurpose room, arrange furniture in a way that divides the room into separate living and dining spaces. A strategically placed screen or curtains hung from the ceiling are simple and inexpensive ways to accomplish this. Make sure the room stays balanced and that the sections or divisions don't fight one another. Area rugs are a great way to define areas and groupings. Small pieces can easily get lost in a large room, so be sure to group them with larger elements.

Shapes can figure in your Feng Shui, and you may well have noticed that when you use sharp angular shapes, particularly on buildings, can cause agitation or irritation, whereas rounded shapes tend to feel more nurturing. Some buildings have employed sharp exteriors – this may give a crisp appearance, but to those in the know, it can also "cut through" any facing buildings, particularly in the direction of the extension of the angle. So for a harmonious environment, be mindful of where you place sharp points or angles.

Feng Shui Your Kitchen

Optimize your Kitchen Organization and Simplify your Life

Kitchens are easily the busiest room in our homes. Whether small or large, a lot of activity goes on there. In larger homes, this is amplified; from cooking and entertaining to a place for kids to do their homework, play board games or work on their arts and crafts projects, it can be easily overrun with art supplies, outdated spices and unused or damaged utensils.

To Feng Shui your kitchen, keep in mind that my rule of thumb is this; as much clear bench or working space as you can manage will give you the same amount of space in your brain when you work in it... But then, that's me. My parents used to say "A place for everything, and everything in its place"... this takes some practise, and is not always possible in such an activity focussed area. When I had young children and needed to be super organised, I made it a rule to have everything, and I mean *everything*, put away in the kitchen for in the morning so that I would not be held up looking for or washing something that I suddenly needed!

This could be very exhausting, especially after a full day's work, helping the children with their homework, cooking and cleaning up, and preparing for another full day to follow. And I would often fall into bed... If I had to do it over again, I would like to think that I could on occasion relax such a rigid rule to make life easier for myself.

So if you have a general plan for where you would *prefer* things to be and you *generally* have them there in those moments when you are not flat out cooking or cleaning or doing something else that is work-intensive, and that on *some* nights there are *some* moments when everything is "where it should be", then you will have a sense of satisfaction in your kitchen.

And of course, if you don't have any children, even if you are working goodness knows how many hours, you can play it how you like...

I would always advise, however, regular clearings and checks in your food cupboard... I usually check all items at least every six months or so...

So you can make this into a **Feng Shui of Food** exercise:

Go through your kitchen and discard anything you don't use, along with any food, spices or medicines kept in the kitchen that are beyond their expiration dates. Then take everything out of your cupboards and drawers, and wash the insides with warm soapy water. Rinse, let dry and replace cupboard and drawer liners with fresh, new ones if you use these.

Alphabetize your spices and herbs (or prioritise them in frequency of useage) and keep them near the stove on a spice rack or in a nearby cupboard on a revolving rack. Store food items that you use on a daily in a place you can easily grab them when needed. Organize your pantry so that similar goods are in the same place and can be found easily when it's time to cook meals. Make sure your children an easily reach items they use on a regular basis, and make sure items such as knives, scissors, and household chemicals are out of reach and secured in a locked cabinet. Utilize airtight (preferable glass or safe freezable) food storage containers to lengthen the shelf life of your foods.

To optimise easy access for tools, **Feng Shui your Utensils** etc:

Store pots, pans and cooking utensils near the stove, nesting the pots and pans together to conserve space. Make sure each one you choose to keep has a matching lid. This is also a good time to make sure handles are securely fastened, so keep a screwdriver handy to tighten down skillet handles or pot lids if necessary. Keep your dishes and silverware near your eating area or your dishwasher to shorten meal preparation or cleanup time. Plastic and glass (healthier and more preferable to plastic) storage containers can be inventoried to ensure each has a matching lid and that they are free from cracks or other damage. Store them near your refrigerator to ease meal cleanup time.

If you have small appliances on your kitchen countertop that you don't use on a regular basis, remove them and store there in a nearby cupboard or pantry. If you have one, use the countertop storage cabinet for those appliances that are used on a regular basis as this keeps them out of site and helps reduce the countertop clutter.

Which means more space – Yay!

Tools For Space Clearing And Enhancing

In this section we cover information on how to use the suggested clearing techniques and tools and provide some ideas as to their uses. I have listed the suggestions for the Space Clearing Tool Kit components and also some Feng Shui ideas and further optional extras together. For quick reference and ease of access they are in alphabetical order.

There are many ideas here, and some of them you can be performed as a maintenance exercise without having to address a full Space Clearing.

AFFIRMATIONS

Positive statements and affirming thoughts greatly enhance the power of a Space Clearing.

Statements of Intent or Affirmations can be used during your clearing process, and there is a separate section on this after this listing of space clearing tools.

However, sometimes we need ongoing practice of a particular affirmation that works at a deeper level within our self to enable change in a no-supportive thought-pattern or behavior that has been of long-standing.

In order for affirmations to work, you MUST word them in a way that your subconscious mind won't resist. In other words, make them believable.

Becoming aware of our internal self talk, or of that inner voice that takes over where a parent has left off, is the first step to changing a negative attitude or thought that has prevented us from getting what we want in life or that has prevented us from having the peace and freedom we seek. Usually that little niggly voice is so swift, so quick when it runs through our mind that we don't even notice it.

Working with affirmations in a regular way can really change the way we think. There are ways to go about it that can reap benefits quickly, but the main keys to know is that any affirmation we choose to work with is believable, reachable, worded in the present tense, and is personal.

ARTWORK and CALLIGRAPHY

Artwork can be a very powerful tool for infilling with positive energy after a house clearing or in enhancing a space by maintaining a certain "tone". Good artwork combines the languages of color, composition, symbology and context and can enhance a space with joy, serenity, vitality, peace, inspiration, healing, soothing, fun, creativity or just plain beauty.

Don't overdo it if you have a few or several really good pieces that can help link your rooms or create links in the mind to nature and aspiration. It can enhance one's breathing, nervous system, mental co-ordination and also allow a focus of thought that brings in higher vibrational energies.

Artwork helps to bring nature into our mind through association, and the eyes drink in soothing symbologies and colors that refresh the brain.

Artwork can be an enhanced form of color healing when balanced correctly.

Happy pictures can enliven a place especially if it has life affirming colors. Be open to discovering the right pictures to give you the best feel to the space you are considering enhancing in this way.

For me and for the purposes here, Calligraphy is meditative writing that incorporates conscious intent to create a harmonious and meaningful positive message to grace a space.

There can be power in some pieces that really supports a space. It doesn't work for everyone, but when you find a piece that feels right to you, it will provide you with much soothing and pleasure. Whether you understand the words or not.

Though I must confess that I always insist on knowing any words that I put on my walls – words have power.

BOUNDARIES

Physical boundaries are clear to see, usually comprised of doors, walls, fences, or signs and markings. Some are easy to monitor, others not so. Locks at doors, solid walls, high fences – all give a clear message. They may say "Keep Out" or they may say "Permission to enter is required". They are not the only boundaries however.

Metaphysically, boundaries represent our ability to guardianship ourselves and our energy. Our home boundaries can also reflect how our personal boundaries work.

Energetic Boundaries are invisible lines of protection you set around yourself – these define what you allow others to do or to not do to you or what you allow others whilst in your presence or with your belongings.

Lack of Emotional Boundaries can allow others to dump on you, lack of Physical Boundaries can allow others to harm you etc, lack of Spiritual Boundaries may allow others to "lead" you or control your Spiritual Path, lack of Energetic Boundaries can allow others to infringe, interfere, bleed, drain, manipulate or steal from you. Your Boundaries can be violated by others, or by *yourself* through your very own thoughts.

Adopting other peoples thoughts ("you should do this/ be this...") will interfere with your own energy fields and chakras.

Identifying and releasing these issues and of becoming aware of what you have allowed, without blaming others, will bring you into a good place of self responsibility and self enjoyment as you experience your own self respect and that of others. Martyr issues will weaken boundaries, as will Religious issues that condemn one to being "less than", a sinner, unworthy etc. Boundaries are not necessarily "the Ego", just the correct nurturing of oneself in this world – others cannot or may not do it for you.

Creating Boundaries for yourself, your home, your work space and even your car can be a challenge, but is so worthwhile. For some people, they think that there should be no boundaries and perceive the world as all one. This is true to a degree on a spiritual level. However, we cannot live each other's lives and the very boundary of our skin indicates our physical separation and individuality; just as we cannot function when we totally merge into others physically, so it is the same psychologically and energetically.

We draw up boundaries when we decide (and follow-up with appropriate action) what we will allow and what we will not allow. Being clear about what we allow or not is primary to creating the right boundaries whether at home or work.

Some we can afford to be a bit lax about, particularly in family, but only to a certain degree. Respect is key to boundaries and expecting respect for them is important for them to operate as such. Some people have a good sense of boundaries. Others, often empathic or sensitive in nature, may find it more difficult to monitor. But it is worth the effort.

Creating energetic boundaries in work can be very effective. Particularly when we decide what we will and will not allow, and we find ways to implement these clearly to others.

Working on your personal energy fields will be of immense help with boundaries.

I can also recommend any of the books by Harriet G Lerner – particularly from her "Dance" series books; "Dance of Anger", "Dance of Deception", "Dance of Intimacy" – for practical ways to make change.

BRASS BOWLS

Brass bowls are quite amazing. I have several, and I use one dedicated to the "burning-off" of toxic energies, as well as other bowls that are for making vibrational sounds to clear energy. Sound penetrates into places that color can have difficulty accessing, so it can be very powerful for getting into spaces that do not get a lot of light and it can work effectively on materials such as rugs, furnishings or other materials that may have harboured inharmonious energies.

BURNING BRASS BOWL

Brass is the safest metal to use when clearing negative or toxic residual energies from a space as it does not hold onto them. "Burning-off" is a powerful method to clear and purify a space. When combined with intent and knowledge you can do a major energy clearing quickly. However, you are working with the fire element here, and must take safety precautions and never ever leave a fire unattended. Also respect the element of fire and its purifying abilities to get the best results. Fire is strongly connected to light as it brings light into dark spaces.

SINGING BRASS BOWL

These Brass Bowls are often called Tibetan Bowls or 'singing Bowls" as they produce humming or "singing" sounds and harmonics, which work very effectively in dispersing built up stagnant energies, and in bringing a different flow of energy into a room. Though sometimes referred to as simply brass bowls, they are often a combination of several types of metals, often and usually made in India by hand. You can gently tap them with the accompanying wooden stick or use the stick to run along the outer rim with consistent clockwise movements until you coax a humming sound. Careful playing can produce a couple of different notes or harmonics. The sounds also help rebalance personal energy fields and can even assist with certain Chakras (these chakras are "energy wheels" and are part of our unseen human energy anatomy).

BUCKET

Whenever I do any energy work, I set up an invisible and energetic bowl or bucket to catch the fragmented energies being released during the session. This is set up to catch and trap the energies, and also to transform them and is placed where it cannot interfere with anyone or any function in the room. I often place a fire that is dedicated to the Light inside the bowl to transmute these energies and to transform them, a bit like an incinerator, only the end result is positive energy that is redistributed back to the Cosmos. You can use a Violet Flame for the same purpose. I have also used a kind of vacuum mechanism to suck up the negative and toxic residues into the bowl and flame. If you do this at home, or anywhere that you are staying or visiting, ensure it is not in anyone else's way, and always, always dissolve it after you have finished with it. For leaving it around may possibly later cause complications for others. So be mindful to clean up after yourself in this way.

BURNING-OFF

You will need a Brass Bowl for this, as "burning-off" is exactly that – you need to use fire to "burn" the energies… I usually combine the "burning-off" with herbs to add extra impact and power to the clearing.

Before lighting, you will have already prepared yourself and will be clear about your intent. I usually direct malign and negative energies to go to the Light or if you prefer, to turn toward the Christ-Light. Burning-off will clear a good deal of unseen toxicity from a space, particularly using clear intent for dross and residue to emerge from furnishings, furniture and other aspects in your clearing. You can use the scripts and ideas in the *Statements to Clear* section as you burn. See especially "*Residues*", "*Fragmented Energies*" and "*Imprints*" etc.

My recipe is to cover the bottom of a medium size brass bowl with about 1-2cm of Epsom Salts, and add you choice of herbs such as white sage, lavender or wormwood etc. depending on your desired result. Then add (carefully) just enough methylated spirits to barely cover the salts. Place onto a fireproof mat or mats, and place in the centre of the room space to be cleared. Ensure that there are no items or furnishings close enough to get over-heated or catch fire. Keep a heavy blanket or other fire extinguishing precaution nearby whilst you perform this exercise.

I will usually place the bowl in the centre of the room, or as near to it as possible. If you are doing a large house, you can do one in each room if the energies are quite heavy or if this is the first clearing you are doing in this space. (Most places only require one burn-off.) If it is a small unit, you can place as close to the centre of the entire area you occupy as possible, still keeping away from flammable surfaces etc.

Stay fully present to the process as this helps to direct the energies out for burning.

When you clearing up after your Space Clearing, you can cover and soak the contents of the bowl in water and let the now-stuck salts-residue soften. Then you can dispose of this down an outside drain, or if this is not possible, down the toilet. Store your bowl for next time only when dry.

CANDLES

Candles signify the bringing and honoring of light – it speaks of inviting the light into one's life, experience and space. It helps to remind oneself of the light that we came from and which we can return to. It helps us reconnect to our self, our sense of the Divine and provides a focus for this. It also introduces the possibility of light "holding" the space for us and assisting us to harness our own divine possibilities.

Lighting candles helps prepare the space for inviting in one's guidance and angelic support. I usually always begin a Space Clearing with the lighting of a candle or of several. Usually lighting groups of 3 candles at a time enhances the power of purification that they bring.

There are occasions where I have lit one or more in each room being cleared. But I have also done very effective Clearings without having them handy, though I do like the feel of candles and the ambience they bring.

Lighting a candle or candles can also be part of your self preparation.

One last word – it is best not to blow out your candles, as this is a waste of the breath which in itself is a creative force, just as a lighted candle is a creative force. Wherever possible use a candle snuffer or remove oxygen from the flame by covering it completely and safely.

CD PLAYER

This can be an essential item for playing Mantras or Clearing Music in a space. If you know how to "tune-in" or intuit, or even muscle test (kinesiology) or pendulum, you can discover the best choice of cd's, mantras or music required and then muscle test or pendulum for the appropriate track to play for each room or space.

CEREMONY

Here's a simplified version of a Space Clearing ceremony that you may want to try in your own home or space to begin to create a kind of respect or sacredness in your life. This is also a great maintenance technique if you have had to clear heavy duty imprints and simply wish to maintain mundane buildup.

Don't ever do this in someone else's place without their explicit permission as this would be an infringement.

First, prepare by cleaning and tidying the space – possibly a mini declutter or after the normal domestic cleaning chores. You can choose to do just one room or the whole home. As mentioned, if possible clear out any flotsam and clutter you have in the rooms or on the premises.

This "ceremony" or ritual is designed to clear out stagnant energy, and stagnant energy always collects around clutter. That's why people who have a lot of clutter may feel so tired and stuck all the time.

Before proceeding it is recommended that you prepare yourself and cleanse your own energy first – you can take a full bath or have a shower, ensuring you wash your hair and brush your teeth. Next put on clean clothing and roll up your sleeves.

Don't wear shoes or metal jewellery if possible. If you don't intend to wash your hair again after the process, it is recommended that you cover it up as energetic debris can cling to hair, which may cause you bother later.

Open a window, so that you have circulation of air in the space. If possible have some flower heads on hand as part of this ceremony together with a candle. Have some good quality hand cream with you and apply some after the initial "Scan".

After centering and connecting to your true Divine Source begin to "scan" the area in this way: Starting at the entrance, go around the inside perimeter with your hand outstretched at heart level, sensing the energy of the walls and furniture from a few centimetres away. If you are right-handed, go anti-clockwise; if left-handed, clockwise.

With practice or sensory sensitivity it's possible to "read" with your hand everything that's ever happened in the place, but to begin, just try to sense differences – warm or cool, nice or unpleasant, sticky energy or clear, thick energy difficult to move in or easy thin energy. Some areas may even feel disgusting! The corners are where stagnant energy tends to collect the most, so they are usually markedly different to the walls in between, and it can feel like putting your hands into unseen cobwebs. Just make a mental note of whatever you feel.

You may wash your hands when you've finished this circuit if you feel you need to.

Next, place a candle in the middle of the space with some picked flower heads around it, preferably of different shapes and colors.

Place them so that they radiate out from the candle. Centre yourself and light the candle, dedicating it to the highest spiritual connection you have, similar to the way the Balinese do when they make their offerings.

Go to the corner nearest the main entrance, and clap loudly a few times into the corner. Start with your hands above your head and move them down to waist level as you clap. Intend with conscious and strong thought that as you do so that the vibrations from your clapping extends right down to the floor and up to the ceiling. Smooth down this new smooth energy fully into the corner and imagine filling the space with this clear energy with your hand. Anchor this energy into this corner.

Next, hook into it with your hand at heart level, and as you continue to pull and spread this clear energy take it with you as you continue to move around the space to the next corner with your hand outstretched towards the wall. Repeat this in each corner, following the same path you took when you first scanned the room by energy sensing.

Clapping may sound pretty simple and straightforward but in fact there's quite a bit to it. Done correctly, it's a very powerful way of dispersing stuck energy in a room. Be sure to get right into the corner, and breathe deeply from your belly as you do it. In fact the whole clap is directed from your belly, done with authority and power. This is not a technique for wimps!

If you want to be really thorough, open up cupboards and clap them out too, as well as any soft furnishings in the room (beds, sofas, etc), which are very absorbent of stale energy.

At first the clapping will sound dull and then, as if by magic, the sound becomes crisper and clearer as you progress around the space. Finally, by the time you get back to where you started from, it should sound resonant and clear. If not - guess what? - you'll need to go round again! Either you weren't putting enough into it, or there was just a lot of stuck energy to clear.

As Clutter makes it much harder work this is why it is recommended to attend to it beforehand.

A word at this point in case it happens to you; it is possible that some people may also have an emotional response when doing this. We can become energetically (as well as emotionally) connected to our homes and in the process of clearing energy in the physical home we are often also clearing energy and a corresponding energetic stuck-ness in ourselves. The tears can be a way of letting go. Just let them happen, and keep moving.

Now – VERY IMPORTANT – wash your hands and arms up to the elbows under cold, running water, to rinse off any energetic debris that has backlashed or ricocheted and become stuck to you while you've been clapping. Then go around the space, sensing the energy again. Most people are able to feel a significant difference.

You can blow out the candle when you've finished, or leave it burning for a while if you prefer after removing and disposing of the flowers. However do not leave it unattended. This is not just for reasons of fire safety but also for reasons of energetic safety. You may also chose to place fresh cut flowers in a vase of water in the room to bring their freshness and color further into the space.

What can you expect after doing this? If you applied hand cream you may have less sore hands with clapping than not using it! Apart from this, people report how much brighter and clearer the space feels and that they feel the same way too. It's like clearing out all the cobwebs of the past.

In the lounge, visitors are likely to comment how different the space feels. In the kitchen, you'll feel happier preparing and cooking meals, which puts better finer energy into the food you eat. In the bedroom, clearer energy can mean better quality sleep, not to mention an improvement in your relationship with your partner and your sex life! In a meditation room, it will clear the space in a way you'll wish you'd have thought of before.

Done regularly, simple techniques such as this can add much to the overall quality of your life. As any six year old Balinese child can tell you, it's just as important to take care of the unseen worlds as the seen ones! And then have a luxurious bath and clean your hair!

CHIMES

Chimes are a beautiful addition to enhancing the energy of a space. When gentle breezes flow, they are stimulated into movement, and when one of their tubular foms connects with another, it renders charming tones and notes.

Some chimes are very small, giving a very high and light tone. Others can be very large, giving a much deeper sound that can resonate for some distance. Some tubes are metallic, though there are also tubes of wood and even clay. Each has its own particular sound, and can bring pleasure to those that enjoy them. Not everyone likes chimes, particularly if they find their sound distracting, but generally it is an acceptable way to move energy and also bring a sound that is unpredictable into the environment, helping the mind to switch off from the expected regularity and anticipation found in most other forms of sound and music.

Do take care not to hang it where it is continually chiming, as this can become a distraction. And if the area is prone to huge gales, position your outdoor chimes where it has some protection – as well as providing protection for your own ears. Unless you wish to double its use to keep birds or animals from your garden patch!

CLAPPING

Clapping your hands can be an effective way to shift energy and move stuck stuff on – you can use it to clear corners of a room as well as energise spaces. Here is the Clapping section extracted from the Ceremony exercise preceding this.

After lighting a candle and mentally (and where possible physically) preparing yourself ...this can include pre-washing and applying hand cream.

Go to the corner nearest the main entrance, and clap loudly a few times into the corner. Start with your hands above your head and move them down to waist level as you clap. Intend as you do so that the vibrations from your clapping extends right down to the floor and up to the ceiling. As in the Ceremony exercise, Smooth down the energy in the corner with your hand, hook into it by hand at heart level, and then continue around the space to the next corner with your hand outstretched towards the wall, pulling the clear energy with you as you go. Repeat this in each corner, following the same path you took when energy sensing.

Clapping may sound pretty simple and straightforward but in fact there's quite a bit to it. Done correctly, it's a very powerful way of dispersing stuck energy in a room. Be sure to get right into the corner, and breathe deeply from your belly as you do it. In fact the whole clap is directed from your belly, done with authority and power. This is not a technique for wimps!

If you want to be really thorough, open up cupboards and clap them out too, as well as any soft furnishings in the room (beds, sofas, etc), which are very absorbent of stale energy.

At first the clapping will sound dull and then, as if by magic, the sound becomes crisper and clearer as you progress around the space. Finally, by the time you get back to where you started from, it should sound resonant and clear. If not - guess what? - you'll need to go round again! Either you weren't putting enough into it, or there was just a lot of stuck energy to clear. Clutter, by the way, makes it much harder work.

In case it happens to you, I will also mention that people sometimes have an emotional reaction when doing this. We are energetically connected to our homes and in the process of clearing energy in the building we are also clearing a corresponding stuckness in ourselves. The tears are a way of letting go. Just let them happen, and keep moving.

Now – VERY IMPORTANT – wash your hands and arms up to the elbows under cold, running water, to rinse off any energetic debris that has stuck to you while you've been clapping. Then go around the space, sensing the energy again. Most people are able to feel a significant difference.

CLEAR DRAINS

This is another metaphysical tool I use, and it can be a very important one, as usually not much attention is paid to this part of one's property. An often unconsidered aspect of energy clearing in the home is that of drains. I discovered this some time ago when energy still felt stuck in the bathroom despite continued Space Clearing. It became apparent that the home I was living in had a buildup on old energy in the drainage system from the shower and sink. This was not just from past inhabitants, but had been challenged because of the amount of energy work I had been doing that had resulted as a result of me clearing my energy systems whilst having a shower. The system had become clogged through the amount of toxicity I had cleaned off, and this all needed flushing away energetically.

The solution was to imagine white light travelling down from each plug hole, each draining orifice, and following its drain line as best I could. I was able to sense which way to send the energy and I followed the lines all the way off the property and even down the road, as there was also a part blockage there possibly from some neighbours.

You can also perform this with your laundry drains and toilet drainage, particularly if there has been illness or stomach problems, as well as all normal sink outlets. It brings a quite different sense to your "wet" areas and helps revitalize your space. Not only through your drainage systems, but the whole of the floor area can feel renewed and refreshed.

COLOR

Color is often best used as a Feng Shui support and as a Space Clearing maintenance tool rather than for actual Space Clearing. Though sometimes including a new coat of paint can certainly lift the feel of a room, particularly if one chooses a paint of suitable color and that is without toxic ingredients (these can affect some sensitive type people).

There is certainly power in color (as discussed in my book "*Secrets Beyond Aromatherapy*") which describes the unseen or etheric colors of essential oils and their subsequent actions.

Light colors or pastels generally enhance and expand a space, and because they contain a lot of white, they bring in more of the energy of light. [Light being a major source of life-force, chi or prana.] This works with the basic hue of the color to bring it to a higher vibration.

Sometimes, a good clean and scrub of paintwork can reveal its original color again, so you do have some choices without necessarily having to go to further expense. Also using certain colors in the materials for furnishings or curtains can bring a new vitality or sense of harmony and order to a room or space.

Here is some information on colors that may prove useful.

White is good for enlarging a space and reflecting negativity, though it can be "cold" when there is too much of it. Pale colors act similarly as their deeper counterparts (ie red + white = pink) though the white brings in more light energy. Greens and pinks are usually "heart" colors and good for feeling nurtured. Blues are generally cooling and give a sense of space. Yellows are often good for concentration or "lifting" ones attitude. Violets or purples generally feel calming and nurturing. Peaches or coral-ish shades are gentle nurturing shades.

Oranges tend to bring excitement and can feel joyful. Deep maroony reds can be quite centering and grounding if used in suitable proportions.

These are just some brief ideas, and it is worth investigating the meaning of color and also what they actually personally "feel" like to yourself before deciding to change an existing color scheme.

CRYSTALS AND STONES

The use of Crystals to enhance a space has been long known. We use Crystals as adornments in the form of jewelry, and crystals are in common and everyday use in our watches, video screens, computers and a variety of other applications. This is mainly because of the ability of Quartz Crystal to bring rhythmic order, store and transmit energy and energetically clear and enhance a space. Used in the home, they are not merely a form or decoration, a curiosity to be handled and examined, or a utility to hold down paper as a paperweight – they are also adept at grounding and enhancing the energy in a space. They bring nature and ancient history in a refreshing form into the home, and are a subtle subconscious reminder of the earth we live and dwell on as well as an energetic form of earth consciousness, assisting us to ground back into the present and into the physical. There are crystals for all sorts of uses and experiences, too numerous to cover here. I write more about Crystals in a separate book and I include the specific Cipher Codes for crystals as well as instructions on aligning them to the new energies we are experiencing.

Generally, the best crystals for the home are those that clear and those that ground, but in actuality, any crystal that makes the resident feel good is the right crystal. Grounding crystals tend to be the Smoky Quartz, Hematite, Tourmalines, and dark colored stones, even flint rocks or granite can achieve the same effect. Granite contains tiny flecks of quartz crystal and has a very natural and energetically warm (cosy) feel to it. Stones or large pebbles can feel very earthy and reassuring, and some people like to have a few rocks or stones clustered together for a tactile experience.

Clearing crystals include Amethyst (especially in the form of geodes which are cave like formations), Citrine, Calcite and Clear Quartz.

Remember that your crystals will not only need periodic dusting or wiping, but also my need recharging as they work energetically to keep your space clear and may eventually accumulate an overflow of energies that prevents them from working fully. The simplest form of clearing for crystals, stones and large pebbles alike is to place them on a sheltered patch of earth to allow them to release and recharge again.

Read more on the specific Codes and uses of crystals in my book on *"The New Crystal Codes"*.

ENERGY FIELDS

Your own personal energy fields may also require strengthening of boundaries or tone. Just as you are working on the energy fields of your personal space, you can also prevent further contamination by keeping your own energy systems clear.

I write more about this in *"Secrets Behind Energy Fields"* (*Energy Healing Secrets Series*) available currently in ebook (Amazon) and soon to be published in hard copy.

ESSENTIAL OILS

We are all aware of the difference that the perfume from an essential oil can make. When used in combination with Space Clearing, the essence, active perfume and unseen colors of essential oils can be very powerful. They can be used for the restoration of appropriate energies into a space that has been treated and cleared.

They can give an immediate shift in energy with the use of the right oil. They provide a welcome atmosphere. They create a mood or particular ambience. And often they can assist with keeping a space clean and clear.

Besides preparation for working with energy, or in providing a different sense in a room, I also use them in conjunction with other tools to ensure that there are no "pockets" of energies left behind and that stagnant energies are truly "moved on".

Most tools are best used in conjunction with several others as each method is excellent in its sphere of action but is not necessarily all encompassing. Which is why I have assembled the techniques and treatments together in this book.

Even the most dedicated of prayers or ceremonies for purification can include the perfume and ambience of oils or incense made from oils or resins of oils.

Essential oils work well when used in sprays, polishes, some surface cleansers, oil burners, and when having baths. To use in a spray, read the suggestions in the section on Sprays.

Though there are other uses as explained in my book *"Secrets Beyond Aromatherapy"* (*Energy Healing Secrets Series*) where you will find many ways that these lovely oils can benefit you and your life.

For house clearing, I find the Frankincense excellent. Other oils such as Lemon myrtle and Lemongrass can assist with electromagnetic smog.

Essential Oils are able to work on many levels, and can encompass many energetic aspects that include the brain and neurology, as well as the Chakras and past issues.

FENG SHUI TIPS

These ideas are great for after a space or house clearing. They help enliven areas or promote harmony. Feng Shui treatments can include the placement of mirrors, hanging mobiles, wind chimes, bowls of petals or blossoms floating on water, flowers in vases or plants in pots, color matching and co-ordination to create "zoned" areas or delineate specific space or room functions, Chinese writings on parchments or in paintings, artworks of beauty, serenity or inspiration, fabrics that inspire gentle sensuality and comfort.

Sensual luxury in the form of materials or tactile stones, ornaments, adornments, decoration and water features – all of which can become a focus to relax, soothe and relieve the eyes and mind.

Some of the handy quick fixes that can improve energy flow in a space that requires enlightening can include:

    Artwork, Calligraphy

    Create space by moving furniture etc

    Furnishings, Fabrics

    Light

    Mirrors

    Mobiles - I love the sound of chimes and cannot have enough of them.

    Music

    Positioning

    Stones, Crystals

    Zen

FABRICS, FURNISHINGS

From a Feng Shui perspective, fabrics should make one feel soothed or calm if in a living area. In this modern day, we sometimes like to combine soothing styles with enlivening ones, and this is purely a personal decision. Overwhelm with clashing and clutter does not promote harmony, but places need to be lived in and not just admired. So where possible, choose quality fabrics and furnishings that make you feel good in your space, whatever its color or style. Particular natural products such as wool, linen, silk etc. Get the best you can when possible, as you will be living with it for quite a while and you deserve the best you can afford. Positioning of furnishings can have an impact on a room or place, so give a little thought to how much you really need, as providing space for air circulation in a room can reduce the amount of periodic clearing it may need.

From a Space Clearing perspective, fabrics and furnishings absorb energies. Easily laundered and cleaned items are preferred, as are natural products. Washing, then, can be part of your clearing protocol. Or regular dry-cleaning – with plenty of airing to remove possible toxic chemicals – are another alternative to removing ground in and resistant energies. Items like mattresses and couches may need different handling, as they are thicker and can absorb and hold more. The Lavender spray recommended for mattresses is useful, as is the occasional Burn-Off. Also consider Scripts.

FURNITURE CLEARING

Furniture and furnishings can absorb the energies of others. If there has been much happiness, this is not such a bad thing. But do you really want other people's energy in and on your furniture? And if there has been unhappiness or trauma, this can be absorbed and slowly released over time unless this is taken care of appropriately.

Dusting alone is insufficient to clear accumulated energies from furniture. Wood and natural products such as wool, linen, cotton etc will absorb energies over time. Though plastic products are less absorbent, they also have an unnatural feel to them and these too can become overlaid not only with the energy of the chemicals used in their production and manufacture, but also with the energy of handling by others.

Sound is a good clearing agent, as is Lavender Furniture Polish. Strong mental or psychic intention can also assist in clearing any inappropriate energies, particularly when combined with the Burning-off exercise and wordage – See Scripts / Wordage. Mantras are helpful too.

GRATITUDE EXERCISE

This is such a positive thing to do when we find we have been overwhelmed by someone else's problems, or indeed when we have been through a difficult time and have recovered enough to move on again. After a trot of difficult times, the brain can almost get used to more of the same, and so it is helpful to remind the brain and the body that there are indeed things to be grateful for. Emotion of a negative kind can settle and permeate our space, so using gratitude can help lift the frequency of a space and place again and help recharge its vitality.

It's quite easy really. You can simply mentally list all that you are grateful for and decide to make listing the good stuff as a habit. Some people find writing gratitude lists helps them to remember what they can be thankful for. Others give their thanks or think their gratitude on the way to work or lying down in bed at night or first thing in the morning. No matter how you do it, it will lift your energy, lift your space and create more of the same – that is, things to be grateful for. This is because it lifts your energy vibration which attracts more of the same.

Filling the space with gratitude after a clearing is also a great way to *infill* the space with *positive* vibes again.

A word here – if someone you know has been through a very difficult time and you know that they need to shift their consciousness, be very wary about jollying them into being grateful for what they have until they are really ready to do so. Loss or trauma requires a period of processing before acceptance arrives. Acceptance is the pre-requisite for change and for true gratitude and appreciation.

HAIR CLEARING

Hair can pick up energetic debris and fragments from the environment. In sensitive people, it also appears to have the ability to feel or signal energy – how about those times when we get goose-bumps over something? Hair is almost like energetic antenna, and so must be cared for.

When we feel gunky, sometimes just showerinr or bathing the body is not always enough, and we all know that cleaner and clearer feeling that we get from letting water and shampoo clear our hair.

But we can't always shower when we want or need to, and there are times when we need to have a handy quick fix available.

So a prepared spray can be a good quick fix, especially when we come home from work and need to refresh and reclaim our own "mind" or to clear our head.

And this is often necessary after Space Clearing or energy work.

Regular spraying with a Clearing spray of pure essential oils and water – lavender is great for this – or special essence combinations can keep your energetic hair pathways clear. Just lift up the hair, spray and gently rub it through the hair, and using your fingers "comb" it through and comb any unwanted energies out. Simple!

HANGING MOBILES

This is an excellent Feng Shui tool.

Hanging mobiles can be found to suit both inside and outside areas – wind chimes can bring a gentle musical ambience to outside spaces that also carry through their gentle sounds into the dwelling. They can act to keep energies moving, to bring the frequencies of sound vibrations into a space, and a sense of space and airiness. Often chimes can remind us of more relaxing times.

Hanging mobiles can have fragments of glass or mirror to refract and deflect any rays of light they might catch. Light itself is a combination of frequencies, and like sound, provide the vibration of movement in a room. Used like this in a mobile it acts to help to harness and maximize any movement of air in a room.

Even mobiles that are simply cut-out shapes or shells or anything that can swirl or look interesting, but essentially that can catch a movement of air will be an effective treatment as long as you are not walking into it, or not overcrowding your space. You can use color in mobiles to bring further harmony into a room, hall, corridor or anywhere you would like to add some visual interest.

A hanging mobile can enliven a "dead" space, as well as add interest to a bland space that would otherwise become somewhat stagnant.

HOUSE-WARMING PARTY

There is an old saying – "Always start off the way you mean to go on…"

Having a House-Warming Party can be a great way to imprint your home with happy and positive energy – depending of course on the sort of guests you invite, and the kind of party you hold… But generally speaking, it can assist in clearing your home's energetic space from previous tenants (or the builders" energies!) and in bringing a kind of "lived-in" feel to it.

Genuine well-wishers and their gifts can impart good energy and bring a sense of "welcome" indoors and out. The preparations for a house-warming also help one focus on setting up a pleasant space for one's friends, and this also helps impart positive "chi" into the space as well as giving focus on the ambience and décor, all of which can be seen as mini feng shui treatments.

Too much or out-of-control drinking will invite not just bad company but also opportunistic and parasitic type energies as well as other nasty unseen hanger-on-erers.

Having a genuinely good time will imprint on the furnishings, joy and laughter in particular being real "feel-good" energy. This can help shift some accumulated dross.

Happy music and dancing will lift the vibrations in the house – well chosen good party music can shift negative energy, whilst heavy metal or discordant "music" will imprint just that: discord.

Thoughtful and appropriate house-warming gifts can also bring goodwill energy from your friends, which are then transferred into the house.

And only ever invite those people who make you feel comfortable or who bring special energy with them – it is hard to keep out what you have invited in, so when inviting, wherever possible choose the best and happiest to sprinkle generous vibes into your home.

However a house-warming party or a party of any kind is not necessarily a full Space Clearing exercise.

IMPRINTS

Some people never travel at all because they don't like sleeping in any bed except their own or feel uncomfortable using someone else's furniture or space. Others will forsake their bed for a while but are always glad to get back to it after a trip. The reason for this is not always obvious but the answer as to why this is so often lies in understanding that human (and other) energies get imprinted into material things as well as into spaces.

Energy Imprinting

Over a period of time you imprint your own energy into furnishings, especially your couches and mattress so when you relax or lie on it, it feels like "coming home" to yourself. There really is no feeling like snuggling into your favourite chair or your own bed, especially after you've been away travelling for a while. A gift given by a loved one can possess not only happy memories but also their heart-felt love and care, and we can contact this again when we hold it.

In actuality, you leave a trail of energy behind you wherever you go in much the same way as you leave a trail of human skin flakes in your wake (you are probably already aware that 80% of household dust is human skin remnants).

Energy imprints (as well as your DNA) can get left in the places you visit and especially in the things you touch. The more time you spend in a place and the more often you touch an object, the more imprinted it becomes.

Some people are able to read different kinds of imprints that other people leave on or in walls, furniture and personal belongings; such as whatever is happening or even has happened in their lives - it's all imprinted there. However, it is not necessary for you to have to be able to do this in order to clear these imprints.

Imprints can not only be from contact, but also from emotional or energetic discharge. A row can leave an imprint. A disaster. A crisis or a trauma. As can a happy event. The stronger the energy, the stronger the imprint. And also the more persistent the consistent emotion or energy, the longer the imprint. It is almost as if an energetic ghost of a film is left behind, recorded on the ethers in space, leaving its own particular vibration.

Enough negative vibrations can override positive ones, and also vise-versa.

For remember that we can leave behind positive energy imprints, those feelings associated with comfort, or happy memories, or good times, or just being cosy in our own little place.

Generally the more absorbent the furnishings, the more we can happily imprint "home" into them. Our intention here is to clear the negative energy imprints and wherever possible set positive and welcoming energy instead in their place.

To remove Imprints, using clear focus and intent visualize washing the space with the Ultra-violet as instructed in that section. I further follow-up with a diluted version of melted Platinum which gently washes through and out. This helps to clear resonances and programs from the DNa of others that may have been left behind.

Read more in the sections on Mattress Clearing and House Warming to get further ideas.

INCENSE

Incense is another ancient Space Clearing remedy, still used by the natives of India as well as some religious groups or other mindful people wishing to clear their space. Generally speaking, incense is regarded as part of their sacred rituals, and is effective in assisting to carry negative or invasive energies out of a space. It combines ancient knowledge of sacred animals and the art of aromatherapy.

Not everyone realizes that the dung of elephants are often used in the making of incense sticks – but further investigation will reveal that this substance has the power to counter electromagnetic interference and to clear negative energies very effectively. The natives use the dung inside or on the walls of their homes to help protect them from negative energy and entities.

It is a strong smell, so wherever possible, have windows open to assist in the dispersal of the smell along with the attached energies and also to prevent build up of smoke from burning the incense sticks.

Besides the usual incense sticks and cones, there are small charcoal burners that you can place special incense gums and resins on that give beautiful aromas and to effect clearings. These can perfume and clear spaces, clothes and furnishings and give off fragrances to suit moods, zones, rooms and their functions.

Incense sticks and cones can also be broken up and added to your burning-off bowl.

INVOCATIONS

Invocations or strong statements can greatly assist in clearing unwanted or invading energies.

The statements listed in this book are favourites, and basically the best commands and statements that have been found to be best appropriate to move the energies to where they need to be. Please see the Statements Section for wordings, scripts and affirmations to assist with clearings and creating change.

JUDGMENTS & LABELS

Visitors can sometimes project a negative thought or judgment on your home space or on something in your home. They may not realize they are doing it, and simply think that their opinion is the right one and that their choice of placement or possession would be something other than what is currently in existence.

On a personality level, this is just opinion. However, on an energetic level, this can create an impact and a Label. Sensitive people may well feel this impact and label, whether they live there or are just visiting, and they feel the effect of the thought that placed it there. You have the power to clear all negative statements, thoughts, judgments and labels placed against anything you possess or live with, even those labels placed there by yourself in an unthinking moment.

"I now safely, easily and completely remove and release all judgments and labels that do not support me, my life or my space."

"All labels and judgments placed against me and my home are now removed and released for now and all time and they have no further power over me."

LAVENDER OIL FURNITURE POLISH

Whenever I can find it, I buy furniture polish containing true lavender essential oil. Not only does it make the furniture look and feel beautiful, rich and luxurious, but lavender is so powerful that it helps dispel negative energies that may have gathered or been imprinted on or into the wood due to the potent purification properties of the lavender. Hand application also assists with moving any unwanted energies, and even though the wood does not appear to be living, nevertheless it seems to respond to the caress of the human hand. So combining the human touch, the wax and the other ingredients in the polish together with the lavender essential oil, you can clear, polish, enhance, beautify and perfume your timber surroundings.

Though not necessarily strictly perceived by many as a Space Clearing tool, polishing your furniture using lavender can be part of your ordering, de-cluttering, clearing and space maintenance plan. And the delightful perfume lasts for ages.

LOST SOULS / EARTHBOUNDS

Success in removing lost souls etc depends on the work done on the self, one's own boundaries, personal integrity, spiritual connectedness, one's own fears and ego etc. By staying neutral and in "service" mode, you can avoid rebound energies. If you don't feel confident, then by all means seek the help of a professional. These processes took me several years to become confident with. In a particularly "nasty" clearing, it took me a couple of days to assess & prepare, and a week to recover, even though I had an assistant to "cover my back" and to ensure that my sensitivity has not held onto anything. But I was particularly sensitive back then. Not everyone is as ultra-sensitive. I provide you some wordings in the Script section under Earthbounds.

The basic principles are to:

Remove;

- others energies back to themselves
- release all toxic, harmful, stagnant and negative fragmented, residual energies & memory imprints – *they are bound by the light, sent to the light etc ...*
- all unwanted and negative thoughtforms are deactivated, disconnected, released in their entirety, geometric makeup and inter-relatedness, *they are gathered together, bound by the light, sent to the light...etc*

MANTRAS / CHANTS

Playing appropriate mantras or chants during a Space Clearing can assist in the process. A Mantra is simply a positive statement, often in Sanscrit – an ancient form of language. It can be very powerful and carries its own individual vibrational energy. Mantras are available as spoken chants from alternate music sections, as well as sung chants. The music and verbal sounds send a vibration that helps loosen and clear any existing vibration that is not of a harmonious or similar frequency or resonance.

There are Mantras, and then there are Mantras – Not all Mantras are appropriate for this sort of work.

I have worked with Mantras for some time, and find them a valuable tool for Space Clearing certain resistant energies. I once did a house clearing that had a lot of "imps" or spirits hanging around, that were eventually cleared by the "Durga Mantra". We had tried several other tools, and had cleared a lot of residual energies and imprints though we were having trouble with these unseen resistant energies.

We found that the continual playing of this Mantra helped to really hit the mark. Not every place needs such deep vibration for clearing, and it is an unusual chant, but with difficult or stubborn energies it may be of assistance. I believe it is available on the internet, though I got my own cd copy when working with a vedic astrology and some Indian pundits.

You can use them in a room whilst working on another room; you can "finish off" a room with them, or in a particularly negative space use them as preparation to agitate the space ready for deeper work.

Abundance and peace mantras will work better *after* clearing a space to imbue it with better vibrations, but mantras such as the "Durga" mantra which is intended specifically for energy clearing played loudly during a Space Clearing will help to clear negative energies whilst also helping to provide a protective vibration.

When choosing to use chants and in particular the "Shiva Mantra", it is wise to consider using the Ganesha mantra first as the Gate-Opener:

Vedic tradition has it that one accesses both Shiva and his consort through Ganesh, the elephant god, echoing a Christian practice of accessing God the father through Jesus the son.

Just remember – quiet harmonious chants are really great for bringing peace to a room. Great for *after* a clearing, but **not** *for* a clearing. I have observed negative energies quite at home in rooms where lots of gentle and harmonious music or chanting has been played regularly.

There can be a certain kind of stagnation that occurs, and the energies are not stirred up enough to support vitality in the room. So they are not necessarily really that effective for Space Clearing. It's best to only play mantras or chants that are specifically designed to move or rouse and clear negative energies. Bajans are a happy form of energizing a space, and are songs of mantra choruses designed to show gratitude and to lift the energy of the singer and the space.

These are not necessarily the only ways to clear negative energies, but the playing of appropriate sounds and music can free one to also concentrate on other tools and areas simultaneously, giving greater impact to your clearing process.

MATTRESS CLEARING

Mattresses are renowned for holding energy – just think about it: we spend almost a third of our lives sleeping or in bed (if not more) and this is often in the closest full length body contact with our bed.

When we sleep on someone else's mattress, it is like being in their unwashed clothes without the benefit of washing them thoroughly, unless the mattress is cleared occasionally / regularly. Remember that a person spends the most time in any 24-hour period in the stillest and most energetically open state.

MATTRESSES & ENERGY IMPRINTS

Everything that happens in a place can be energetically imprinted, even in the walls and furniture, and mattresses usually get more imprinting than most other things. Not only are they usually made of very absorbent types of materials, but they also get the greatest degree of close personal use.

Regular turning of a mattress can help to some degree, but nevertheless, energy gradually seeps through unless you cleanse regularly or when necessary, particularly if someone else will be using the mattress, or if one has been through a very trying or difficult time, and had sleep or nightmare problems.

Never discuss your problems in bed. Why? Because that's what gets imprinted, and then you go to sleep in that space, with your problems swirling around you all night long. If you must discuss issues with your partner before sleep then move to another place, preferably not in the bedroom at all. Keep your bed as a clear space for sleep and intimacy. And NEVER sleep in the same bed with unresolved arguments between you if at all possible. You'll be engaged in astral wars all night long that do long-term damage to a relationship. If you can't resolve an issue between you before the end of the day then it's best for one of you to sleep somewhere else in the home that night and work through the problem in the fresh light of the next day.

Even past relationship energies can accumulate, which can affect the positive moving on of a new relationship. I would suggest if possible that you get a new mattress for your new relationship, if you want it to have every chance to succeed.

Failing that, there are two solutions to that I can offer;

Solution 1 - Lavender Mattress Cleaning – I knew of a little man in the city I lived in who would wet-dry clean mattresses using a mixture that had Lavender essential oils in – the difference this made was amazing! Not only did the mattress smell really good and clean afterwards, but all of the little niggly bits of negativity and energetic residues magically disappeared! It was like having a brand new mattress again. Highly recommended if you can track down your own local man.

Solution 2 - Thwacking & Whacking -

This is a great way to "shake-out" these soaked in and locked in energies that no longer belong in your sleeping space.

Its best to start this with an open window so that there is some circulation of air. Allow several hours for this process and Be Prepared for lots of "stuff" to come out.

Peel off the bedcovers, and put into the wash – or have fresh bed linen ready for when you have finished. Use an object such as a cricket bat, baseball bat, a thick piece of stick or even a rolled up umbrella for this.

Drag your mattress outside the house if you can. If this is not possible make sure that you have windows open and start thwacking the mattress with your stick, bat, or other hard object. This will act to vibrate the energies out. When you've done one side, flip it over and do the other side.

You will probably be able to see the dust flying around. You might even smell stuff from the mattress, but be sure that there will also be energies you can't see flying out. So if you are doing this indoors, do not stay in the room afterwards.

Leave the window open so there is still circulation of air. You can light an incense stick and / or spray with a lavender essential oil spray then or when you return later, as its best to leave things to settle - and then come back a few hours later to do a quick once-round with a vacuum cleaner.

And that's it. Except that you may find you need a bath or a good shower afterwards.

You can do this every few months to keep your bed feeling fresh and clear. It's obviously not as good as buying a completely new mattress but it's the next best thing, and because it's not a complete solution it means that some of your energies will still be embedded there, so it will still feel like "your bed".

METHYLATED SPIRITS

Methylated spirits is often used as an essential help with the "Burning-off" exercise. See this section for full instructions. Obviously store and treat with care as this is a flammable liquid.

MIRROR

Mirrors are a popular Feng Shui tool, and a favourite is the eight sided mirror with I-Ching markings on it sometimes called the Bagua. This can be quite small, yet effective due to its markings. Sometimes a space calls for a larger mirror.

Large mirrors are not really good for promoting peaceful sleep and rest in the bedroom, as they can disturb the energy and create too much reflection and movement in a room that requires peace, calm and serenity in order to relax in preparation for sleep.

However, they can be very effective when it comes to dispersing or moving energies in a space. They can open and expand an area, they can bring in more light, they can reflect more light.

When it comes to enclosed and small work spaces, or where one has to work with their back to the door, they can be very helpful to repel and also protect.

When one has a door at their back, or an open space that can be entered without any warning, this does not allow one to relax into their activity or work as part of them is continually on guard or unknowingly alert for someone coming up on them from behind. And when they do manage to focus on their work and forget about this, they can be surprised and a bit shocked when someone enters unexpectedly. This does nothing for their energy and nervous system, and may build up into stress. It also means that they may feel "spied" on, or even "stabbed in the back" and generally feel unprotected.

Energetic boundaries can be compromised, and even weakened over time, which can also have an affect on one's natural defense system which is connected with the spleen and immune system.

The mirror comes into its own in such publicly-open or energetically confining spaces. Not only can it seem to bring a bit more added light and space, which is the least of its benefits, but it also serves as a warning sign for when visitors arrive behind one.

When placed appropriately, you are pre-warned and can see when someone is approaching, and so are better able to prepare yourself for a disturbance to your current task.

It can also send back negative energy that is approaching from the rear, particularly when directed toward you personally. So it is a handy self protection tool in these situations.

You can also combine this with other space protection methods to enable you to work better and more happily in difficult and confined circumstances.

MOBILES

A well-known and easy favourite for decorating a room and for assisting in energizing it are Mobiles. These are decorative hanging constructions that have several branches which can hold a variety of decorations, and can be placed inside or outside of a house or home to add to it.

Suitable mobiles are those that catch any breeze, and that have refractive surfaces, such as tiny mirrors or crystal pendants. Mobiles of birds, butterflies or flowers, where appropriate, can soften and energise a space, especially if positioned to catch a breeze or the shift in energy when a door or window is opened.

Mobiles actually help not just to demonstrate the movement of air, but also to help stimulate it further. There is more on these in Hanging Mobiles.

MUSIC

Music and sound can be a very powerful and effective energy mover due to the penetrating capabilities of the vibrations of sound. Varying sounds or types of music can produce diverse effects – both with instruments and genres. Some instruments that can help clear and activate a space include Tibetan Bowls, Metal or Crystal Bells, Crystal Bowls, drums, Flutes or whistles as well as good old hand clapping.

Though playing meditation type music can be very soothing, it doesn't help to break up energy that has got stagnant. I have been in spaces playing lovely gentle and even "holy" music that is laden with dark, heavy and toxic energies.

A careful choice of some active music such as party type music that makes one want to jump up and move – though not heavy metal, rap, or head-banging stuff as these don't have the range of vibrations to create the variety needed to shift energy – and that has a happy feel to it can help blast stuck energies. A few minutes burst (especially during workshops when there has been a lot of mind focus and concentration leading to a sense of sleepiness or apathy or overwhelm) can break up and enliven the space again. If doing a "burning-off" I suggest you do this beforehand.

MUSICAL / SOUND INSTRUMENT

This is such a large area, as there are so many types of music, so I will attempt to confine things. Music and Sound can come in all shapes and sizes, tones and decibels. We often choose soothing sounds to relax our nerves, bodies and energy fields and lively sounds to encourage action or to express.

In Space Clearing, the peaceful flute or harp will not dislodge and clear old imprinted energies. To really move stuck, stagnant or toxic energies from any space requires loud and lively music or deeply-charged powerful sound such as the Durga Mantra. I have cleared spaces with lively renditions of the 1812 Overture, and during workshops on energy have used energetic rock and roll or popular music as well as lively bajans (mantra choruses). Naturally I also later combine it with more soothing sounds to settle the refreshed and renewed energies, but the point is that active and energetic music can clear a space a lot quicker than hours of peaceful tunes.

Don't be concerned about creating a noise of distraction – just watch what happens when the Chinese celebrate their New Year and bring out noisy drums and even crackers!

When you are aware that you are breaking up old energy that was stuck there in order to move it out, then you begin to understand the action you require to do so. Relaxing peaceful note to reset the space again can follow later.

Use whatever instruments you feel will move energy to clear the space - maybe include bells, cymbals, maracas, whistles, clapping, loud music of practically any sort (except heavy metal and songs of misery or unhappiness – use your common sense here) and of course, the Durga Mantra.

OBJECTS

Walls, furniture and objects can act like an energetic tape recorder for events that happen in a place. Trauma can be buried or absorbed, as can memory and intention.

Gifts too can hold energetic attachments if given with ulterior motives. Some things can be given or offered that have unseen energy conditions or ties, even if it is only a hidden obligation or intention. Some things can be given with the hope that something else will be reciprocated. If you are sensitive, you will feel this energetic tug even though you may not know where it comes from. And for some people it can act as a bit of a drain on their energy, as it keeps them somehow connected with the sort of person they might be better off without.

Even though any object or gift is made of just ordinary materials, after all, so you wouldn't think this sort of thing would be possible. But it is. It is not the object itself, but the meaningful energy attached to it. However, this is quite simple to clear once it has been recognized. You can always return the gift, or dispose of it in a way that does not bring you back into contact with the giver, or do a space clearing on the gift if it is too valuable to dispose of or destroy, and you can separate yourself emotionally and energetically from memory that doesn't serve you.

The Ultra-Violet metaphysical exercise can be helpful in clearing any residual energies attached or absorbed by any objects or structure. Also see the Scripts section.

ORBS

Orbs are an interesting problem. When these are indicated for a clearing, it is not that these are the positive orbs of light that are known to be from unseen helpers or advanced and caring consciousnesses that are sometimes picked up on photographs. The ones referred to here are those found in the home and that are usually the sort of "spying" orbs that have been planted by another, whether knowingly or not. If you have ever heard the saying "I wish I was a fly on the wall" then you will understand what an orb is intended to do – it is a kind of feedback mechanism, like a remote monitor, intended to watch and note what is happening in a given space. Particularly strong minds, even psychic minds, can send an orb to a place without realizing it, and this can become the conduit to attempt to connect or "see" what is happening in someone's place. Whether they can actually see or not is not the issue, but the installation of an intent to discover or identify what another is doing is an infringement.

Someone with a strong mind who really wants to know what is going on in a particular place or space can inadvertently set one of these up, which can have disruptive impact on a space. Having had someone in your home or even your bedroom gives them the mental picture to be able to place an orb there.

Without sounding paranoid, this is a definite possibility if you feel a bit unsafe in your bedroom. Rare though this is, I have included it for a thorough clearing experience for you. There is a Statement for this in the Statement section.

PAINT

This is one of my favourite and most powerful Metaphysical techniques. It is the application of Intent, imagination, thought and focus. This aligns the energy of that which we are focusing on into the structure of the space we are working with. This can be performed for your home, your office area, your car, or anything you own. It also allows an area for infusing and clearing with the Ultra-Violet as mentioned later in this section.

Begin with painting the surfaces after cleansing – or as part of the quick clearing – this technique can accomplish a lot in any space. Using Gold energy like applying paint is the most powerful I have found so far to combine clearing and strengthening. I see this as part of the reclamation, refreshing and reenergizing of a space. The usual procedure is to mentally "Paint" with Gold all of the walls of a room first, ensuring that there are no gaps or spaces left behind, then proceed to paint the floor and the ceiling. Next use Ultra-Violet until the energy in the room feels clear. Continue room by room, and finally, all the way around the outside of the apartment or house that you occupy.

You only have the right to address the space you occupy and live in, for you infringe and transgress when you take it upon yourself to interfere with another's living space – unless specifically requested to do so. This interference can come back on you in some way, so do take care to honour others choices.

This amazingly powerful technique of painting with Gold can be applied to any space and area. For best results, always follow it up with the Ultra-Violet as listed later.

PORTALS

This is not a common clearing process, but vital to clear if they are present. Portals are like an unseen access point to a place, space, frequency or energy. Let me explain it like this – when we watch TV we open an invisible portal to whatever it is we are watching and its associated frequencies.

This is also true for certain programs in our computer and also with video or wifi games.

It's a bit like when we open a program in our computer and it comes up as a window – showing an icon whilst it is open. It is accessible as long as the icon is showing open. Until we close the app, icon, program or window down, feedback and feed-through will generally still be available. Because we can see the icon or app etc, we know when to close it down. In real physical life we can turn off the TV or computer, but in energetic space, inter-dimensional, unseen space and even in our head space, the programs can still operate unless we are mindful to turn these off consciously.

When the modem for our computer is on day and night, there is continual feedback and access for the internet and email. So energy portals can be a temporary access or they can be a permanent access.

I have worked with children who could not sleep at night, and people who did a lot of computer work who had similar problems. When I taught them how to close down these portals to their imagination-ings or to their work problems, they were able to settle down to sleep easily.

Closing down the portals left behind from others will also stop static, feedback or access from some unseen place or dimension from interfering in the here and now.

PYRAMID

Being of a somewhat sensitive nature, I found in the past that even though I had cleared my space, it was still possible for my sleep to be disturbed through a variety of energy interferences. I had to learn a lot about my own energetic boundaries, or lack thereof, and set about rebuilding them. One of the things I found really helpful was to energetically protect my sleeping space until my energy fields were strong enough to do so themselves. (Trauma can damage not only nerves, but also make one even more sensitive than they were before – and it can take some time to recover and rebuild.) I found that working with the Pyramid really aided me.

When I have finished painting my walls in Gold, which I of course do periodically, and on occasion even whilst I am lying in bed, I might add, I erect a Pyramid directly over my house. It usually has four sides and a floor to it, and the house sits right inside this. It is usually of pure Gold (energetically speaking of course), and its aim is to protect my space and support me.

I stumbled upon this when I first tried placing one over my bed to protect me.

Being the extremely light sleeper that I was in those days, I really needed something like this to help me. And it did. So then I decided to try it over the house. A very psychic friend of mine came to visit one day, and remarked that they could see the Pyramid over my house when they were down the road! I was more than surprised, originally thinking it was all in my mind, but this convinced me otherwise.

I have since made my Pyramids not quite so obvious (I don't really need to attract attention from wandering ghosts or imprints do I?) and it is just as effective.

I quite like the idea of sleeping in a golden Pyramid at night, one which allows me to breathe peacefully. Try it!

I always, always finish off my clearings with this golden Pyramid over the house, as it helps set the new energy and seems to imbue the whole place with such a supportive, strengthening and beautiful tone.

RECLAIM / RESET / INFILL

After clearing imprints, decluttering and removing negative energies from any space or place, we need to reclaim the space again and to energetically *fill* it with the sort of energies that *we* want there.

This is *essential* to prevent recurrence of the same issues again. Now is the time for you to use Feng Shui enhancement, or check down the list here:

- Essential Oils
- Soothing Music
- Flowers
- Color
- Luxury fabrics; silks, linen, velvet, whatever feels luxurious to you
- Artwork or decorative items without overloading
- Reposition existing placements for a better "feel"
- Affirmations to Clear By can become Affirmations to Change By

RITUALS / CEREMONIES

Rituals and ceremonies were very much a part of Space Clearing, but things have changed and we have evolved to a more immediate and "being present" type of clearing. We are in an age where we can now work with more immediacy by working with the power of our intent rather than depending solely on a pre-set format of a set of actions that "creates the change". However if it makes you feel better or more comfortable to go about clearings in a ritualistic way, then work with that. One can gain more confidence when one can progress to a more spontaneous sense of what is required. If you can be centred, and able to rely on your own sense of intention and of "holding" the space, you may well discover your clearing more effective than depending on a format that was not of your own creating.

If it suits you better to work with rituals, then devise what feels right to you with what you know and what you feel comfortable from the techniques in this book. I would also suggest that the parts you incorporate into any sort of ritual would include self preparation and the lighting of candles.

Regardless of the above, there is a section on a form of Space Clearing ceremony or Ritual to give you some basis to work with. You might also use the section Statement Section which includes Script and Wordage ideas.

ROOM BY ROOM

Room by room treatment means addressing each room and clearing it one at a time before moving on.

You can have candles and music or sound playing in other rooms or in a central position in the house whilst you undertake this. Keeping the internal doors open is usually preferable as it allows the energies to circulate and gives less likelihood that the person performing the clearings absorbs what is being released.

When "painting" your rooms to strengthen its boundaries and to provide an intended area to clear, ensure that you leave no gaps in your painting. You can use a large brush, or spray paint or however you want to apply the energetic color to your walls etc.

Paint each room as instructed in the Paint section, addressing walls, floors, ceilings, doors etc. Do each and every room, hallway.

I often finish by painting the outside of the house all around to ensure it is one whole property or entity.

This is then extended to the fence or boundary line, and includes paths, garden etc. If you are ultra-sensitive, I suggest you also put a coating over this outside gold that blends it in with your surrounds and does not draw attention to the bright shiny gold. This also tends to deter unwanted and inquisitive energies.

SAGE STICKS / HERBS

Smudging has been recognized as a Space Clearing tool for quite some time and white sage appears to be the best for most purification purposes and for neutralizing and transforming or converting crappy or negative energies as well. This lovely herb brings a delicate smell even when burning.

It can be used for "Auric Clearing" as well as for removing imprints and energies from furnishings and your home environment.

Other herbs that can be used for "burning-off" can include wormwood for clearing parasitic energies, and lavender leaves and seed-like flowers for rebalancing energies and bringing harmony. Others worth considering include basil leaves for clearing argumentative energy and for protection, as well as rosemary leaves for protecting and for clearing energy as well as enlivening the space. There are more but this is a good basic list to play with.

SALTS – SEA / ROCK / EPSOM

Epsom salts are great for using in a bath to cleanse your energy fields, and for using with the Brass Bowl for "burning-off" toxic energies. See the section on "Burning Off". You can also use salts to clear off certain crystals. Magnesium salts can be used for:

    Burning

    Baths

    Soak Objects

    Supports Energy Fields As Magnesium

SATIN and BEAUTIFUL FABRIC

This can be seen as another Feng Shui tool.

Texture can add or detract from a space. Note the difference when you wear rough fabric as opposed to something of high quality or of a nurturing texture or feel to it. Many find that they do not feel as comfortable with polyester or other manmade fibres for their sheets, but enjoy the feel of cotton or a natural fibre that seems to allow the skin to breathe.

This ability to affect the sense of touch can be coupled with the esthetic to bring another dimension into a space. Touches or articles of silk, satin, textured wool that are coupled with complementing or harmonizing color can impact more than just visually on a space. The energy of a fabric can work its magic on the space of a room!

Besides the luxury of the feel of special fabrics, the visual aspect can achieve many things. Beautiful tapestries, wall hangings, furnishings, curtains etc can do more than "lift" a room – they can give a certain feel, a certain ambience, a certain tone – they can make a huge difference even with just one or two well chosen pieces. Imagine a very plain room, one that is tidy and organized, but very bland. Place into it one or two complementary items that suit the room, your taste and your budget, and that make you feel comfortable and nurtured.

Some ideas that can help you enhance your space:

>Color is projected into the Aura of a Room

>The Luxury of the Fabric can Enhance a Space

>The Eyes, senses and Touch are Fed with the chosen Fabrics

>Placement is important to Feng Shui the Room

>If it is a favourite scarf or Pashmina, you get to enjoy it daily

SMUDGING

Smudge sticks are usually a bundle of herbs bound together so that the herbs are easily hand held. You can light them easily from a candle flame or use matches. And you can use your intent to add to your smudging, such as imagining any feelings of depression, or any past arguments being bound to the smoke and being carried out of the room. It also helps to have an open window or two to allow movement of the smoke outdoors, carrying negative influences or energies with it..

Once there's a flame blow it out so that the smudge stick is smoldering, not burning. What you are looking for is to get curls of smoke, not to set the smudge stick on fire. (Note of caution: Do not smudge while infants, pregnant women, or people with respiratory diseases are in the room.)

When smudging objects, such as crystals, you can hold them in the smoke. If you're smudging groups of crystals you can fan the smoke over and around them.

When you are smudging a room, you can first walk about the perimeter, giving special attention to the corners and the places behind any doors. You can continue into the room and wave the smudge stick in a slow circle until you feel you have covered all of the space in a room. Some like to take a large feather and fan the smoke throughout the room.

When smudging yourself, you can use a feather to fan the smoke so that it flows over or touches all parts of you. It may assist when you smudge areas where you feel there are blockages or where there is or has been any physical, emotional, or psychic pain.

You can also smudge your clients if you are involved in energetic healing work.

Wherever possible, have a fireproof receptacle nearby to extinguish the smudge stick in when you've finished. You can use a shell or glass or ceramic dish, or bury the tip in a bowl of sand. Or you can use a tiny amount of water. Always, Always make sure that a smudge stick is out before leaving it.

SOUNDS / NOISE

Clapping, beating a drum, shouting, and other sounds that may seem to be noise have an action of disturbing "stuck" energies.

Using the force of sound can loosen energies from where they are embedded in the space or corner of a room as well as help to release embedded energies, for sound penetrates through matter easier than color does. Cement is hard to be penetrated in this way, but most household furnishings can benefit.

Afterwards, you can imbue, refresh, enhance or replace these old or stuck energies that have been removed from the space or area with positive, uplifting, harmonious or happy and enjoyable sounds. Refer to section on Musical Sound.

SPRAYS

In a 32 oz. spray bottle filled with distilled water, add a total of 20-30 drops of any of these blends. Or make up your own blend mixtures. Here are just some ideas...

Purifying/Strengthening – mix into spray bottle Grapefruit, Rosemary and Tea Tree oils.

Energizing/Harmonizing - mix into spray bottle Lavender, Geranium, and Bergamot.

Revitalizing/Invigorating - mix into spray bottle Clary Sage, Lavender, and Peppermint.

Calming - mix into spray bottle Lavender, Chamomile, Orange and Sandalwood.

General Face and Room Spray Ideas

Rosewater is a lovely spray, suitable for so many things. You can dilute it into distilled water, and spritz through your hair to remove any clinging residues, or your face and neck when doing any cleaning up or disturbing of any furniture or items. This can also be used a a room or space spray.

You can also add a couple of drops of lavender essential oil to your rosewater spray for added effectiveness.

This is good as a general room spray, and is usually safe for most non-delicate fabrics. Though I would suggest you always check before use. Always avoid spraying near the eyes, this naturally goes for any spray of any kind. And be aware that spectacles may need a wipe and clean after, as the fine mist can leave a very fine film of oil on the glass.

Sprays are excellent for a quick "lift" to a room or space, and can be very effective in reducing the amount of residual energies caught up in the atmosphere and held in the fabrics and furnishings.

They also bring their own aroma or fragrance, and this not only works on the sense of well-being but also works on the neurology of the brain and body, adding extra benefit from the use of the spray. See Essential Oils.

And of course, there is the energy clearing spray that you can use for clearing your hair as mentioned in the Hair Clearing section.

SPRING CLEANING

As mentioned earlier, a thorough spring cleaning can go a long way toward clearing old and unwanted energies. Being mindful that you are working on energetic and unseen levels as well as physical levels will assist you in this, as energy follows thought and intent.

Always follow your clean up with a bath or good shower, cleaning the hair as well. All cleaning cloths etc and cleanup clothes straight into the washing. The removal of cobwebs, fingerprints, grime, dust, dirt, etc can be accompanied by the refreshing of the space with a consciousness that is enlivening all it sees and all it touches, bringing fresh energy and vitality to all areas encompassed in this way.

Unless a residence has deeper and more serious issues, a declutter and spring clean can achieve a lot.

SYMBOL / MANDALA

Symbols and Mandalas are a large subject in themselves. In space clearing they are usually purpose-specific.

Symbols

Symbols are a form of language, and it is a language that enters directly into the brain, providing messages and impetus along the lines indicated. Symbols may appear to remain in the background, but over time they can imprint upon the subconscious through visual channels. They may be embodied in an image, in an abstract sign, in a glyph, part of a geometricity, in an illustration. Symbols can be painted into works of art or used in religions or societies. They surround us and we often don't see them.

They are used in advertising and media, as logos or even as unseen background indicators. Symbols can be used directly or subliminally. Positively or negatively.

In the home, for rest and recuperation, recognize what symbols you surround yourself with, question them and if you ascertain that they are positive for you, then retain and use more consciously. Otherwise, dispose of those things that do not support you, your family, the ambience of your home or your peace of mind. Peace symbols can impact, just as violence or crude symbols can. Animal symbols of strength, astrological symbols of planetary impact, flower symbols of healing, religious and hypnotic symbols of martyrdom or war – learn to recognize.

Choose symbols that mean something positive to you and that indicate the direction you wish to move in wherever possible.

Some positive symbols to work with for success, family etc can include:

. Elephant – with trunks held up

- Ducks – in pairs
- Swan –
- Horse – strength
- Bee – honest productivity
- Gold coins – wealth

There are many more to play with. Have fun exploring...

Mandalas

Mandalas are a form or organized artwork, usually of a mostly symmetrical pattern. They can be based on the basic foundation of triangles of 3 sides or segments, square or 4 segments, 5, 6, 7, 8, 9 etc each having a different feel to the basic patterning and each meaning something different. Building on this with shape, design, symbols, color, position and intent can render some beautiful works of art that can incorporate action, intention, truth, transformation, inspiration, awareness, nurture and beauty.

Mandalas come in all sorts of styles, patterns, designs, compositions and even substances. Many are in the form of painted or drawn artwork. Others can be in the form of intricate designs and symbology in fine colored sand as in the Kalachakras built during ceremonies. They can be used for meditation, contemplation, inspiration and admiration. Protection mandalas can be employed to help keep a place safe and clear. Each can have its own unique purpose.

TRAVEL SPRAY

Travel sprays are handy for personal refreshment, clearing Hotel rooms, realignment of one's energies after travelling different time zones, and assisting in minimizing the dross or residue accumulated from many different types of peoples who are experiencing their own journeying. They are also handy for energetic clearing in work place situations. Some good combinations can include Shell Essences for self-care, Flower essences or Essential Oils. See section on Sprays.

TV, COMPUTERS

These devices can be conduits to other places, spaces and unseen dimensions. Imagination operates on another dimension to our physical 3D and once accessed, can leave an access or *Portal* open. These usually are best closed down after use or at the very least, at night before sleep to allow for rest. You can always chose to reopen them, but stay mindful that what you open and access needs to be closed down after. Using wifi can allow energy waves to act as carriers of energy too, so if possible, turn off wifi receivers at night to better allow restful energy in your home.

ULTRA-VIOLET

This is another powerful Metaphysical Space Clearing technique that I use often. The color has a very high vibration and can be used to transmute heavy toxic energies when directed clearly and with positive intent.

Having energetically 'painted' and outlined the walls and space with Gold, I now mentally shower or spray the energy and essence of Ultra-Violet into the whole of the area, often in a sweeping pattern, until I have covered the entire area.

I note the dirty or stuck specs that blink and wink out that are the result of the Ultra-Violet doing its cleansing work, and the stuck lumps and bumps that eventually give way to the easy flow of this Color energy. If there is a particularly resistant spot, stop the Ultra-Violet and proceed to use a Neon Green energy until it is clear, then go back to the Ultra-Violet until the space feels clear and smooth. I usually paint a room and clear it in this way before proceeding to the next room.

VACUUMING and SWEEPING

Though this is not usually considered a Space Clearing tool, nevertheless, it has its place. What many people don't realize is that there are often invisible low-grade energies that fall onto the ground. Or get carried in on our shoes or socks (or feet if we go without shoes or socks). Taking off your shoes at the front door can reduce the amount of low-grade energies carried inside, but it doesn't stop the negative bits of energy we pick up from outside from falling down off our clothing or bodies.

Clairvoyants have "seen" these low grade energies that can be like spiky "tumble-weeds" or clumps of dusty crap, sometimes greenish, sometimes grey or murky brown. It is thought that cats can sometimes see these, and try to deal with them in their own way.

If you really want to make this a powerful cleanse, you can imagine that your vacuum cleaner is sucking up all the little nasty balls of energy and contamination that have dropped down off surfaces, coats, shopping bags, second hand goods, in fact anything, even stuff that has gotten caught up in hair, and it is being sucked into the vacuum bag.

But also is being held inside the bag, and is not being blown out the other side to be redistributed around the room again. Imagine a kind of energy bag or container inside the vac, holding the energies, to be thrown out safely when you have finished.

Another visualization is to imagine an unseen cable from the vacuum bag that takes the low-grade energies directly through to a flame of light – this flame of light destroys the negative aspects of the energies immediately and converts it into fresh air and fresh light.

When you are sweeping up, you can do a similar visualization – you can imagine that as you sweep, you are painting the floor with light with your sweeping broom or brush, and that all the dirt and dust collected is being "decontaminated" the moment it hits your little dust pan or dust collector. You will be surprised at the difference in your cleaning.

Have fun with this.

WALLS

Walls can hold residual energies, particularly imprints of past explosions of energy or emotion. Wooden wall paneling seems to hold more than plaster, concrete seeming to be more impervious to energy permeation. In some old homes, there can be layers of energetic imprint that has gathered over the years.

Many people can neither sense nor feel these energies, but the more sensitive types can. They obviously won't be a problem to people who do not feel them, but if you are sensitive, they may affect how you function or the tone of enjoyment you experience in a certain space.

It is obvious to anyone that new walls, clean and fresh, give a very different experience than old ones, and can also seem to affect the space that they encompass.

Renovations may reveal not only the inner workings of a wall stud, but possibly trapped energies from long ago – to the sensitive.

Consider this too, that children are more sensitive than adults, as are pets, and to take note if they have difficulty sleeping or if they demonstrate discomfort in some way during repairs or renovations. This can be a clue as to the possibility that some old energies may need to be cleared out of the environment.

Washing down or repainting some walls may assist to some degree. However sometimes things may need to be addressed at a deeper level.

Clearing out imprints and energies is a sound move, using music, sound, incense and other ideas in the Statements section. After that I suggest you use the Paint metaphysical protection exercise for best effect. You may also treat floors in the same way.

WASHING & CLEANING

As discussed in the Declutter section, washing can be a form of cleansing, so when doing the laundry, be aware that the water is not only cleaning from physical dirt or debris, but is also clearing unseen energies that have clung to clothing or have gotten trapped in the fibres.

Never underestimate the washing of towels, curtains, chair covers and cushions etc.

Curtains that cannot be washed or it is not appropriate to wash can, where necessary, be sprayed with an appropriate clearing spray (see the section on Sprays) or dry-cleaned or simply taken outside to be shaken and hung in the fresh air for a time.

When washing surfaces, be aware that you are collecting and disposing of not just dirt but also tainted energy debris.

Don't allow too much filth to gather in the water before replacing it with fresh water to continue cleaning.

You may choose to add a drop of essential oils in your wiping down water. Lavender is good, and some people have added a couple of drops of Rosewater, Vanilla essence or Citronella oil if they don't have Lavender to hand.

Wiping down of surfaces with a safe essential oils solution can help to remove old energies and even imprints

Oils such as Eucalyptus, lavender, tea tree, orange etc are usually very effective, but you should always check on whether it is safe to use a particular oil on the item or surface you intend to clean.

You can also be aware that as you move your hand over a space, its energy too, is clearing the space as it goes, so when possible, be aware of your hand movement as it covers the area. Combine this thought with the water and cleaning solution, and of it clearing the space and any negative energies that were being held there and depositing all in your bowl or bucket.

Always give your hands and arms a wash after cleaning up like this, to remove any bits of missed energies or accumulations you may have picked up in the cleaning and clearing process yourself.

You may want to check your face, neck and hair as well, or give yourself a spritz with an essential oils spray such as Rose or lavender oil, or rosewater, to remove any "splashed up" energies or residue.

Of course, not everyone is ultra-sensitive to energy debris, but if you are, then it is handy to know what you can do for yourself. Often many sensitive people require a shower or bath after doing a regular house-work type clean-up.

ZEN

Zen – simply means to reduce things to their function in a way that is pleasing. Living without the extraneous and unnecessary can give a sense of space and spaciousness, and provide an easy energy flow. It does require discipline for many people and can also help simplify life.

If you like having "things on the go" like me, this is not always easy to achieve. Having said that, I like having my living areas tidy before I go to bed at night, as I enjoy seeing "surfaces" and "less" when I get up in the morning. This also helps prevent the buildup of accumulation and the stagnation it can lead to.

Metaphysically, Zen intent brings order and simplicity not only to the physical, which can be seen immediately, but also to the invisible. Order is the opposite of chaos.

Chaos can be a fun thing when wanting to dance crazily or intuitively, and can be very healing. However, later one usually feels the need to return to order again, having been invigorated in this way. Both aspects are required in order to live a balanced life.

Choose which is your predominate way to rejuvenate.

Try them on to see which gives you most pleasure and support.

Zen – Simplicity – the beauty of function and form.

Statements Section

AFFIRMATIONS TO CLEAR

Statements to Clear Your Space

AFFIRMATIONS FOR CHANGE

Statements and Affirmations to Change Your Life

Affirmations to Clear

Scripts / Wordage / Knowledge

This section contains Statements of Intent to help you to clear your space appropriately. However, to make the difference from just speaking a simple affirmation and instead to create a very real proclamation of change, it is important to know the Secret ingredients to really bring this about.

To add power to any Statement, it is essential that one be aware that the use of the outward Breath to "seal" the statement and to give power to the spoken word will make a huge difference to the outcome. The breath itself is a *creative* power, and the voice and spoken word helps to seal the *direction* of that power. So when making a verbal statement of power, immediately follow it with a strong outward breath to help to "set" the inherent command in your statement.

When you have identified what is affecting the energy or ambience in your space, this knowledge can be used to go to another level that is not just physical or material in order to clear any unwanted energies or residues of energies.

Knowledge is often power, and when you can identify an issue, then you are better equipped to do something about it. Harness this knowledge and create a statement that gives clear instructions as to what you require in your clearing.

Invocations or statements can be quite helpful in assisting you with your focus and intent, as they help first to clarify intent, then to add extra power to your intent through your spoken word.

Some people really like working with statements as it calls on the added inherent power of the spoken word as a vibration that enforces and supports one's intent when used in integrity. It is best to avoid coming from ego or emotion when doing any of these, that is, by staying in a "neutral" (non-emotional) mindset yet remaining clear as to the purpose of your clearing - and in this way you can avoid any backlash that ego or attached emotion may allow back in.

You can prepare your statements, script or scripts beforehand. Scripts are simply the writing or listing of what you want to clear, together with your choice of phrasing. Some ideas are included here.

Though not essential, some people prefer to do this in a kind of ceremony when doing Space Clearing, using the wordings as a kind of ritual. An invocation implied here can be a kind of prayer or a command. No matter which way you do it, be clear energetically beforehand.

When dealing with unusual matters that you might encounter in a Space Clearing, having the appropriate wording gives you quite an edge, and will furnish you with the confidence needed to really make a change in your space.

In the statements, the use of the term "the Light" means the energy of light and love. When referring to the Greater Light, this is intended to mean the Source of Light, which is the ultimate transformer of things negative or dark.

By merging your command with correct knowledge and clear Intent, and you have a powerful combination. Then simply hold this space until you feel the shift of energy or that things have changed the way you want. Continuing to use the breath can also be useful and quite powerful in these exercises, by imagining that with each fresh breath in that fresh new energy is being brought into the space in accord with your statement, and with the outward breath, the old stale, undesirable or toxic energies are being released.

ALWAYS, ALWAYS allow time for each statement to have its effect. If necessary repeat the statement several times until you feel it working or completing its task.

You can pendulum or finger test to ensure that each statement you use is completed before moving on to the next.

These are a guide for you to work with and include many of the problems encountered personally;

DRAINS

For more information, see the previous section on Drains.

"All drains and drainage systems in and underneath this property are now flooded with clean clear pure light, they are cleansed and cleared from all harmful, old, negative and unwanted energies and they become transducers and transformers of negative to positive energy, moving and clearing out in a way that does not harm the environment. Thank you, thank you, thank you."

EARTHBOUNDS & LOST SOULS

Earthbound beings are simply souls that have become trapped and have not seen the light. It is not your job to act as the light (though for some people this can be a calling) so you need to be aware that all you need to do is imagine a door of light, see it high up above the house or over the nearest church and instruct that the earthbound being / soul is sent to the light.

Do not allow argument, just keep holding the space and seeing the light, and the door of light that is part of it so that they can see it too.

When I come across any earthbounds, I usually ask the Archangel Michael to assist in moving these souls on.

This is a similar procedure for lost souls too.

You can use the following to assist:

"I now ask for the help of the Archangel Michael to assist in moving on this soul to the Light, to be met by loved and familiar ones, who will care for them on the next stage of their journey. This soul no longer belongs here and is now assisted in whatever form it needs to leave this place and go to where it now belongs. With thanks. So be it, so be it, so be it."

EMOTIONS

The clearing of emotions may need to be done several times when one moves into a new home, as layers of emotion can become embedded in walls, ceilings etc and may only progressively clear or emerge for clearing as each layer is cleared. It all depends on the previous inhabitants. If you wake up really tired and feeling old because your home was previously owned or shared by someone elderly, this is a good way to clear aging issues or fears.

"All residual and absorbed negative emotions are now gathered together by the light, released and sent to the Greater Light for Transformation with harm to no-one. All emotional residue and imprints that do not belong here and that no longer support the health and well-being of this space and the people who live here are dealt with the same way. Thank you, thank you, thank you."

ELECTRICAL / ELECTRONIC ENERGY IMPRINTS

"I ask that all electrical and electronic imprints in this space are null and void, rendered harmless and that their frequency is changed to one that can no longer interfere with the peace of this place. With thanks, so be it, so be it, so be it."

It doesn't hurt to obtain some electrical frequency neutralisers, such as the Orgone devices currently available. This will help prevent future toxic frequency build-up.

There are devices for phones now too.

Also check the position of meterboards and electricity junction boxes to ensure furthest proximity from sleeping quarters etc.

ENTITIES

One needs to hold a space of no-fear, and working purely with the Light, with confidence stand your ground.

You may choose to call on Archangel Michael who is the protector from the negative whilst with his help you instruct:

"All Entities are released from this space, they are bound by the Light and sent to the Greater Light for transformation. With harm to no-one and in peace."

FRAGMENTED ENERGIES

Fragmented energies can be from many sources, and this is the opportunity to gather up any loose energies or fragmented thoughts and dispose of them safely.

"All fragmented energies are now gathered together by the Light, they are released from this space and bound by the Light and sent to the Greater Light for transformation. With harm to no-one and in peace."

GUARDIANS

When moving or relocating there may sometimes be an energetic issue over territory. I write more about it under *"New" Home – Relocation.*

A basic request to ask permission from the Land guardians when arriving can be: *"Land Guardians of this place and territory, I ask permission to live here without harassment, as I come in peace and wish no harm."*

HOARDING

"All energies that are holding fast in this space whether through pain, fear, constriction, suggestion, lack, anxiety, self-sabotage, guilt, shame, blame or any other negative emotion, energy or issue, are now dissolved, and energy flow is now given permission to restore, reveal, remove and heal.

Items that no longer support and are no longer required or current are now freed up to move on to their rightful and proper place, and those things which do support are now welcomed. This space is now open to receiving the greater good again, easily, safely and without harm to anyone. Thank you thank you thank you."

IMPRINTS

"All imprints that have become enmeshed in the energy and frequency of this place are released safely and they are bound by the light and sent to the Greater Light for transformation, never to return. All intent of harm, hurt, fear, pain, loss and grief are now powerless and are completely removed for transformation as stated. So be it, so be it, so be it."

OTHERS BELONGINGS

"All gifts, belongings, second-hand items, handed-on items that carry energy or connection that is not supportive or enhancing of this place are now cleansed and cleared of all low-grade energies, emotions, ties, hooks, obligations, unseen contracts and they are purified completely. What does not belong here is returned or passed-on to its rightful place. What does belong here that was contaminated is now purified and all benefits and any good intentions are now restored free from energetic ties. So be it, so be it, so be it."

ORBS

"I now close down and deactivate any and all Orbs in this space. They are cleared and sent to the Light for transformation with harm to no-one."

PORTALS

"I now close down and deactivate any and all Portals in this space. They are closed down until they are further required and consciously opened by myself again. With harm to no-one."

RESIDUES

"I now clear all Imprints, all Toxic Residue, and Negative Dumpings and all Residual Energies from this Space and from ...the Furniture, furnishings, walls, doors, floor coverings, cupboards, wooden items, curtains, mattresses, clothing, gift items, **easily, completely, and safely.**"

THOUGHTFORMS

Thoughtforms are usually a collection of thoughts that can dictate how things will run – these can be positive, such as the thoughtform for a design or a song, but they can also be negative and upsetting.

They have been known to create dizziness, and as they may move around a bit in a building, one can even walk into them so to speak and feel like you've been suddenly hit on the head.

These need to be moved on as they can interfere with energy flow, inspiration, health and clear thought.

"Any and all negative Thoughtforms are now removed completely from this space, in their entirety and totality, and they are bound by the light and sent to the Greater Light form transformation, never to return here again. So be it, so be it, so be it."

Affirmations for Change

For those of you who wish to enhance and clear your inner spaces, here are statements and affirmations that can help you to focus and to begin to clear what is no longer required or what blocks you. Some of the statements also assist with self transformation.

There are many ways to work with affirmations and if you have the time, writing your chosen statement out repeatedly can really help to shift any stuck blockages that have prevented its truth from being in your life.

When working with kinesiology (instructions for self testing are in *"Secrets Behind Energy Fields")* or suitable energy work, I find it more effective to work with these statements and include an intent for "100%" - this makes it easier to test whether the statement is cleared of all blocks and is fully true, rather than more true than not true – if you are at 51% with something, you are more in agreement than if you were only 49% with something – that 2% difference gives a totally different reading, and you are only just in agreement with whatever it is. So claiming 100% as being in agreement with a statement makes a much stronger truth.

However, it is all your choice. In all statements listed, you can insert the 100% yourself.

You can also play with these statements, pick and chose what you feel you need to be aware of or to work with: you might want give yourself permission, or you might want to feel safe about something, or you might want to feel successful at something – have fun working and playing with these. Let them inspire you to allow more into your life as well as letting go that which you no longer need...

The Statements

Where possible include your own name in your statements – this helps to strengthen the intent too. Adding "100%" as mentioned to statements for serious change.

It is easy for me ... (your name) to clear what is now no longer needed or no longer loved

I .... (name) lovingly express my own truth as I connect with my inner wisdom, now and always.

I am relaxed within myself, and I easily flow with life

I am 100% willing to safely and easily release old and stagnant thoughts from my life and heart

It is 100% safe and easy for me to release old and stagnant thoughts from my life and heart

I ... 100% release old ways of doing things and I willingly embrace new and better ways that support me and my life

It is 100% safe and easy to let go of that which no longer works for me, no longer supports me, or harms me or hurts me and for me to fill the space with that which makes me happier to be me

I ... lovingly spend quality time with myself every day, and with those I love when I chose to do so

I give myself permission to explore and express my individuality in ways which support me and those I love, without harm to anyone

It is safe and easy for me to enjoy myself and my life

I am now 100% free from compulsive behavior and I now choose better and wiser

I am an open channel for the Universe to support me

I ... am 100% deserving of success in my life and in my heart

I ... 100% believe that happiness is my birthright

I ... am 100% willing to give myself permission to fully live my life and to enjoy it

I allow myself to be me, and not to live the lives of others

I am responsible for myself first, I am not responsible for everybody else

I now know how to take care of and nurture myself, and I can do this easily

I am able to balance my giving and my receiving to allow Universal Flow into my life and home

I deserve to live in peace

I deserve happiness and I can be happy

I now allow happiness and peace into my life with ease and plenty

I live a bountiful life

Life supports me; I support me

I can stand up for myself, and I do so without harm to myself or others

I am responsible for my own happiness, and I can set my own boundaries

I choose to only allow those things into my life that support me in the direction of my true journey and purpose

I now align myself with a joyous energy

I now allow good things into my life and into my heart

It is easy to be serene

My home now supports me and nurtures me

It is easy to care for my home and for it to take care of me

I have great pleasure when I care for myself, for it frees up others from having to do so

I appreciate and I am appreciated

I am grateful for all the good things in my life and this gratitude gives me joy and more good things

My home is now filled with peace and love always

I now safely, easily and completely remove and release all judgments and labels that do not support me, my life or my space

All labels and judgments placed against me and my home are now removed and released for now and all time and they have no further power over me

I am worthy of being the best that I can be

I am worthy of having the best

I am non-judgmental and allow this in others

Order abounds and reigns in my life and home

I am grateful for all the opportunities in my life

I welcome opportunities and good fortune easily

It is safe to be alive

I allow positive change into my heart and my life easily

Secrets to Serene Space

WHAT NOW? WHAT NEXT?

Having cleared and cleaned the space, it should begin to feel lighter, clearer, more balanced. Serene. Happier even.

Unless we have already put in place the things that truly support us, however, it can feel a bit like a blank canvas. Some of us may require a feeling of nurturing or beauty to really feel "at home".

In effect, you have scoured and cleaned and scrubbed the place clean energetically. Now what?

Now is the time to consider what the space and its occupants require to provide that added sense of harmony or vitality or pleasure, depending on the room's functions.

What do we now need to feel a sense of space for expression or for the movement of fresh energy to flow or for a renewed sense of vitality?

For a sense of possibility, success, freedom, serenity, safety, security or whatever it is that you require to really support your living and your life?

Many invest in artworks of beauty and inspiration – these greet and please the eyes as well as impact on the brain and nervous system to subconsciously support us.

Others choose well-designed furniture. Some choose furnishings, paying attention to what feels or looks right to them in the designs, fabric feel and the colors. Others fill the space with sound – the music of their choice, or nature calls such as birds.

Some choose to imbue the air with the play of etheric and exotic scents of essential oils or scents, or combine the beauty of color and perfume in flowers.

Still others place plaques with inspirational wordings or mantras to inspire the conscious and subconscious minds. Or install a water feature, or a fish tank, or a bowl of water with floating blossoms.

Some bring in more light in the form of candles or lighting features, or replace curtains or remove blinds. Some simply move objects into a sense of a better placement in the new space.

Here is where Zen and Feng Shui practices can enhance and assist the Space Clearing.

There are so many ways to further enhance your purified and cleared space, and so bring more joy into your home and living experience.

Go back to the list of Tools for Space Clearing and see what now appeals to you.

This is the opportunity to paint across the blank canvas of your new visual and etheric space.

Enjoy!

Easy Repeat

So now you have cleared your space and are enjoying the new feel... imagine if you will, that you may not have to go to so much depth every time you want to "lift" the energy of your environment...

To make it easier and to help keep the energies at a level that supports you, you can choose to do some things that reduce the amount of work a full clearing would require. However, as energy is always changing, and as we live life fully, we will still need to check in on the atmosphere and ensure that the energies are clear from time to time.

But by now you will be starting to develop a better sense of when something is amiss and requires your attention.

All you really need to know is that you can now energetically clear your space and place. Skip or scan quickly through the list to see what is required, do it, and Voila! Back on track again.

I hope you enjoyed the information here, and I wish you well in keeping your place serene, smiley, sacred, soothing, sensational – whatever it is that supports and nurtures you!

Further Information

Questions & Contact Information

Please feel free to write to the Author with your success stories. Your questions are welcomed and every endeavor will be made to answer each one. This book has been compiled from answering the needs of clients and through personal experience whilst training and practicing in consultancy. If there is anything more you wish to know about, then **YOU** are invited to contact me with your most burning questions as to energy, life, relationships, depression or self help, self individuation, self-identity, development or responsibility.

In return, your questions will be answered and when there are enough questions, a free copy of the resulting new book will be sent to you as a "Thank You"!

To send your question or comments, email:

admin@myrasri.com

If you would like more information about this or any other book or meditation or to be kept informed of the publication of the New Evolved Chakras book, you can email her direct, or register your email for newsletters at www.myrasri.com

Or follow Myra at her Amazon Author page:

http://www.amazon.com/author/myrasri

ABOUT THE AUTHOR

Myra Sri was born in England and moved to Australia in her twenties with her then husband and two children. As a sensitive person, she maintained a spiritual leaning.

Moving out of her unsupported marriage and leaving behind her naivety in religious faith she embarked on the reconstruction of her life and the discovery of her true identity.

Continuing to work in the mainstream business, accounting and media industries, she found that connecting with other people further inspired her on her own self development journey and assisting others in their journeys led her to naturally gravitating to the healing professions.

Undertaking extensive training and study she became an energy healing practitioner and kinesiologist. Qualifying as an instructor in several modalities, she subsequently discovered where there was a lack of teaching and understanding and set upon research and discovery, resulting in her own unique advanced workshops which have been taught around Australia since the early 1990's. These continuing experiences led her to develop her own innate skills and supported her in re-membering her healing skills and psychic abilities.

Running her own private practice since the late 80's, Myra remains an avid explorer and student of evolving ways to heal and support the soul and spirit.

She wrote her first book in 2006. Regular trips to the UK concerning family issues, until both her parents died and after further teaching and training returned to Australia, whereupon Myra was inspired to document and write about her learnings, including the energy shifts with oils and crystal healing and the new Chakras.

She embarked on the *Energy Healing Secrets Series* in 2012 which fulfils part of her role as a Transformation Agent. The *Energy Healing Secrets Series* is presented to assist in self help, self healing and spiritual mastery.

With the advent of the new era energies and her discovery of the new evolved Chakra systems, she has written and developed the *New Evolved Chakras Workshop series* which includes the new Earthing Chakras, the Psychic Body Chakras and the Signal-Survival Chakras. The discovery of these extraordinary Chakras have also been confirmed by other spiritual teachers and psychics to be instrumental in everybody's healing process and the book on these Chakras is soon to be published.

Myra provides a safe and attentive healing space for her clients and students, and works multi-dimensionally, enabling major energy and spiritual shifts. Her focus is on the Soul and spirit. Considered a resort for difficult or complicated situations, she has often been referred to as 'the Healer's Healer'. She works multi-dimensionally, enabling major energy and spiritual shifts.

About Myra's Workshops

Some of Myra's workshops include:

Past Life Training – Navigating Soul Journey and Genetic Issues and Karma safely

HygienEthics Series –Working With Energy, Living With Energy, Being Energy, Protection HygienEthics, HygienEthics for Therapists, Advanced HygienEthics

Navigating Life in a Changing World

Muscle Testing Basics

Crystal Workshop

New Evolved Chakra Series - New Earthing Chakras, New Psychic Body and Chakras, New Signal-Survival Chakras

SECRETS BEYOND AROMATHERAPY

The beauty and power of Essential Oils has been known to us for thousands of years, from Ancient Indian healers to current day aromatherapists.

Few were aware of etheric Colour Codes of Essential Oils.

Until now!

Essential Oils, like the Chakra systems, have evolved and Come of Age.

Their abilities have expanded and they are now poised ready to assist us all as we work with and move fully into the new energies of this new Era.

Come on a journey into the astounding colours of oils; see how they interact with human senses and subtle body anatomy. Learn their impacts and the unseen implications with the Soul and incarnational aspects. Discover which Chakras respond best, and which energy system is most enhanced by their actions. You may be pleasantly surprised!

The basic etheric body colours of the human energy systems appeared to have undergone change. Even the Main Chakras are responding differently to colour and vibration. It would seem that no longer do most of us reflect (and often poorly at that) the basic opaque paint-box-type colours previously associated with the seven basic colours of the rainbow – some of us are now able to reflect more glorious and colourful hues and iridescences from and through the auric layers and chakras when balanced correctly.

Living in cities can prevent some of these new hues and their tints from shining within and without, as the electromagnetic smog and pollution can lower the frequencies to a paler and poorer version. In these times it is becoming more important to reconnect back to nature, the land or the sea, purer energies, higher vibrations and natural remedies whenever and wherever possible to sustain us. And the essential oils is are part of this remedy.

The humble oil along with knowledge of its inherent etheric colour codes and abilities will further enhance everyone's experience of the nature and the knowing that is held within each loving oil and hidden within the etheric world itself, and will further enhance and amplify all of your current benefits when used with the increased awareness.

Recognize the New Roles that these amazing gifts from our Planet are playing right now.

Explore the Etheric Colours of over Thirty Essential Oils. Learn their Secrets.

Find new and powerful ways of working with them.

Spend time with them. Let your choice of Oil reveal to you further hidden information to assist you with your client or with your own personal transformation.

Work with Essential Oils in ways you've never done before!

Amazon Reviews:

A treasure of energetic information

Thrilled with the content of this book and I have read almost every aromatherapy book there is

I wonder why this book is not used as a textbook

SECRETS BEHIND ENERGY FIELDS

When we have good health, we really do have a huge asset at the ready – there is no price to be placed on it as from our good health so many positive things can arise. When we are exhausted and tired through dealing with other peoples issues, emotions and energies, we are cheating ourselves of our true destiny and life journey.

Nobody lives as an entire isolated and energetic island to themselves. We are all social beings and part of life is social interaction of some kind or another. Which also means energetic interaction - the contact that takes place on those unseen levels, yet we can still feel their action and their impact.

When we don't know where our energy goes, when we work with others closely, when we are faced with emotional or traumatic scenes, when others think it is ok and acceptable to explode around us, when we think there must be something wrong with us because of what we continually encounter in our life, we need answers to what is happening, and what we can do about it!

Learning to navigate through life in energies that are less than positive or harmonious sometimes requires outside information or help. And all you really need to invest is some of your time and energy to become your own energy guru and healer.

Here is a collection of techniques, exercises and tools that are proven energy strengtheners. Selected from the many workshops I have taught on this topic are easy, effective solutions and understandings for anybody who is involved with other people and not coping as well as they could.

You can begin to reclaim your own identity and autonomy again, and easily recognise who and what has been affecting you with the easy to follow instructions and ideas.

Be successful and happy, protect your energy and let good health and good energy be your positive foundation.

Amazon Reviews

"Thanks to this eBook, I am teaching myself to rise above the conflict at work... these life skills are priceless!"

"This is an excellent, practical, down to earth book that is filled with simple techniques to get in touch with yourself, your own energy, what is affecting it and then how to do something about it."

"I found this book very informative and the techniques were simple and easy to follow. I would recommend it to anyone who does energy work."

SECRET TRUTHS – HEALTH & WELL-BEING

If you are doing everything "right" and yet there is something that cannot be explained that compromises your experience of life and vitality, you may well need to look deeper... look past symptoms, past the apparent, past expecting a pill to fix what you can do for yourself.

Exhaustion and tiredness can have several causes. Compromised health can often find us resorting to the local doctor or our health food store. Energetic and emotional impacts, toxicity or damage from others may need to be addressed and resolved separately (*"Secrets Behind Energy Fields"*). We are not just our body, we are not just our mind, we are not just our emotions. We are an amazing combination of all of these and more. The being is an amazing orchestration of matter and that unseen life-force; spirit. When one part is hurt, the other parts are affected.

Here in this book we look at important and often hidden contributors to compromised health and equilibrium as well as very real yet often hidden aspects of tiredness, exhaustion and depletion of energy. Many are not aware of simple things that one can fix for oneself. Nor how easy it can be to make a few mental or verbal changes for oneself that creates a positive impact on health outcomes.

If the nervous system is compromised by amalgam fillings, or lack of hydration, or unresolved issues, then results will be way short of what is possible. If the mind is blocked through lack of simple yet essential nutrients, and is not even aware of essential requirements for health, if a person cannot recognise when they have adrenal exhaustion and how their thoughts can feed into this, what chance does one have of full recovery?

If inflammation is causing pain in the body, what can one do about it? Here is a mix of experiential physical advice and of energetic and spiritual tips from a long-standing expert on body-mind-spirit issues, written to help those who wish to find answers to their problems or symptoms on the *physical level* themselves.

NEW CRYSTAL CODES

Since the huge energy shifts of recent years, frequencies have been updated in many areas. The discovery of the new Evolved Chakras has demonstrated that we are all in a process of upgrade and re-alignment. This includes not only the human subtle bodies but also the energetic frequencies of oils and crystals.

This book contains clear instructions on How to Align your Evolved Crystal to the New Incoming Energies.

The author shares her knowledge on the new Crystal Codes and Ciphers, as well as how to read where your crystals energies are at and how to align them with the new Era frequencies.

You will not find this knowledge anywhere else.

This little book also has everything you need to identify the different functions and powers of Quartz Crystals and much, much more.

You will learn about how to connect to your crystal, how to care for it, code and program it and how to use it wisely.

You will find in these pages ideas that will inspire you to love and journey with your chosen gem.

You will also learn how to identify various types of crystals, some metaphysical properties, sets of crystals and learn the difference between an Isis crystal, a Record-Keeper, a Lemurian and much more...

Make the most of your willing crystal and harness its energies for the new energy shifts right now!

This is cutting edge information and the time is ripe to re-energise your crystal.

SECRETS Beyond
Aromatherapy
CHAKRA HEALING SECRETS
ETHERIC COLOUR CODES
TRANSFORMATION SECRETS
Behind the Invisible Etheric Codes
of Essential Oils
MYRA SRI
Secrets Behind
Energy Fields
BECOME YOUR OWN ENERGY GURU
RECLAIM YOUR ENERGY & VITALITY
SECRETS to
SERENE SPACE
SECRET Truths
Health & Well-Being
HEALTH TRUTHS THAT EVERYONE SHOULD KNOW
TOXICITY AND THE NERVOUS SYSTEM
SECRETS BEYOND NUTRITION
Resolve Exhaustion and Tiredness NATURALLY!
Recognise Obstacles to Health and Vitality
Body-Mind and Emotional Impact
MYRA SRI
The NEW
CRYSTAL CODES
Align Your Crystals
To The New Energies
CRYSTAL CODES, CIPHERS AND FUNCTIONS
FOR THE NEW ERA
MYRA SRI

www.ingramcontent.com/pod-product-compliance
Lightning Source LLC
Chambersburg PA
CBHW050537300426
44113CB00012B/2140